TVET*360*:

The Full Circle Story,

Volume 01

Nana Naz-Khan

TVET 360: A FULL CIRCLE STORY

First edition. November 4, 2024.

ISBN: 979-8227121325

Written by NANA NAZ-KHAN.

Contents:

Chapter 4: The TVET Variants

Chapter 5: The TVET 'MAESTRO'

Disclaimer

All evaluations conducted by TVET360 are for educational purposes only. These assessments aim to provide insights and facilitate comparisons across different nations. They are not intended to degrade, belittle, or criticize any country. We respect the unique strengths, cultures, and challenges of each nation.

These evaluations are based on valid and reliable data to provide accurate and meaningful insights. For the most accurate and personalized information, individuals should consult local experts, official sources, and consider the specific context of their situation.

Foreword

*By **Dato' Ts. Dr. Mohammad Naim Yaakub,***
Former Director-General, International Organisation of Colombo Plan Staff College, Manila.

Former Director-General, Polytechnic and Community College Department, Ministry of Higher Education, Malaysia.

There are many books about TVET in the market. From the person wishing to be acquainted with the subject to a doctoral student wanting to focus on a particular aspect, there's something for everyone.

So, why write this book, another addition to the plethora of available publications on TVET? The answer becomes instantly obvious once one starts reading it.

Rarely does a book cover the breadth and depth of TVET, let alone traversing across time and place. This is definitely TVET 360, as I would frame it. A comprehensive, one-stop book that covers almost, if not all, on anything TVET.

This book offers a comprehensive, panoramic view of TVET, traversing time, place, and context—a true TVET 360. It spans foundational concepts, historical roots, and modern applications, exploring TVET's evolving role across sectors and cultures. From practical insights on program design to policy implications and international comparisons, this text addresses TVET's role in building adaptable, future-ready workforces. It's designed for students, practitioners, policymakers, and administrators alike, providing them with essential knowledge and insights to deepen their understanding and appreciation of TVET's transformative power.

The author brings nearly 30 years of experience in planning and operationalizing TVET. This depth of expertise, from high-level strategy to on-the-ground application, gives him a complete understanding of the field. As a seasoned planner, he traces shifts in technology and the workplace, forecasting the future landscape of TVET and its crucial role.

For anyone seeking to understand today's workforce preparation or looking to stay updated on TVET's impact, this book is essential reading.

Author's Note

Do we truly understand TVET? Is it even possible?

Our leaders often advocate for emulating TVET (Technical and Vocational Education and Training) practices from abroad. Numerous benchmarking visits and exercises have been conducted, particularly in Europe, to reform and improve our local systems. These efforts, made in the name of progress, carry the hope that adopting successful models will drive meaningful change at home. Yet, despite the time, resources, and effort invested, the outcomes consistently seem to fall short. There is a noticeable disconnect between what we learn abroad and how effectively we apply it in our local context.

That's the reason for this book.

Welcome to TVET360. I'm Zainal Azhar ZA (Pen name: Nana Naz-Khan), with over 30 years of experience in Malaysian Polytechnics and Community Colleges. Together with my AI assistant, Maya, I'll guide you through the many facets of TVET, as we explore what makes a vocational education system not just functional, but truly exceptional.

Striking the right balance between vocational and academic education is essential for creating a skilled, adaptable workforce. TVET, however, remains distinct in its emphasis on work-readiness from the outset.

At TVET360, we explore the intricate world of vocational education and training, engaging in insightful discussions, offering expert analysis, and sharing real-world stories. Each piece is crafted to inform and inspire a diverse audience—from industry professionals and educators to students and policymakers.

The vision of TVET360: A Full Circle Story is to provide a comprehensive, multidimensional, panoramic view of Technical and Vocational Education and Training, demonstrating its role in shaping careers, driving economies, and enhancing lives globally. We focus on delivering discussions that explore the profound impact of TVET on both individual development and economic growth. Additionally, TVET360 features expert national analyses, breaking down the success factors of leading systems like those in Germany and South Korea, offering valuable lessons and strategies for other regions.

Volume One will focus on the fundamentals and history of TVET, tracing its evolution and role across various regions. It will culminate with a deep dive into the German Dual TVET System, widely regarded as one of the most successful models globally. This chapter will lay a solid foundation for understanding how historical and socio-economic factors shape TVET systems, providing invaluable insights for policymakers as they seek to adapt and implement effective strategies locally.

It all began with a burning question: *What makes TVET in Europe, especially in Germany, so highly regarded?* Why do we refer to it as the "gold standard"? Initially, I sought to explore these elements for my own understanding, but as my research progressed, I felt compelled to share these insights. I began by documenting my findings on a blog, but as the depth of my research grew, it became clear that a book was the logical next step.

As I delved deeper, it became clear that understanding TVET's success requires a comprehensive approach. Replicating foreign models isn't enough. We need to look at TVET from a broader, more inclusive perspective—a holistic view that examines every aspect, from policy to implementation. This realization inspired me to create the concept of a 360-degree strategy: TVET360, a framework designed to evaluate and improve TVET from every angle.

Join us on this journey through TVET360, where each chapter is a step toward understanding and harnessing the power of vocational education.

Let's reflect, engage, and transform the way we view TVET together.

Nana Naz-Khan
(Zainal Azhar ZA, PhD)

The TVET WORLD

Chapter 1: The TVET World

The world of TVET is vast—so vast that we often view it in fragmented pieces, and this, I believe, is part of the challenge we face today.

TVET is a complex term, and without a comprehensive understanding of its full scope, policy planning can fall short. The big picture is essential. Just like the parable of the blind men and the elephant, we must see and appreciate TVET in its entirety if we are to create effective solutions.

> *"TVET is more than just training; it's a comprehensive learning pathway."*

The acronym TVET stands for Technical and Vocational Education and Training, and it is built upon three key components:

1. Technical Education
2. Vocational Education
3. Training

The following are three components are the basis for understanding the world of TVET. To allow us in understanding this further, Maya has come up with a table to clearly show how the three components stand:

In essence, TVET encompasses the learning experiences that offer a choice of study, leading to almost immediate employability. As the image above illustrates, these components may either blend seamlessly or exist separately. What's more, you, the learner, have the freedom to choose your path. Whether you aim to become a baker, a graphic designer, or an AI technician, TVET offers diverse opportunities.

Component	Focus and Interconnection	Typical Outcomes
Technical Education	Emphasizes the application of scientific and engineering principles. Includes **training** in specific technical skills and procedures as part of the curriculum.	Graduates are prepared for careers requiring technical expertise, such as engineering technicians, with the ability to apply theoretical knowledge in practical settings.
Vocational Education	Prepares individuals for specific trades or professions through a combination of theoretical knowledge and **training** in practical skills relevant to the occupation.	Graduates are ready for immediate employment in their chosen field, equipped with both the necessary practical skills and the foundational knowledge of their trade.
Training	Though embedded within technical and vocational education, training can also stand alone as short-term skill enhancement or upskilling for specific job roles.	Improves job performance and competence in specific tasks or technologies, beneficial for both initial career preparation and ongoing professional development.

TVET emphasizes the development of hands-on, practical skills directly applicable to the workforce. It integrates theoretical learning with experiential training, allowing learners to engage with real-world tools, equipment, and scenarios specific to their industry.

When discussing skills in the context of education and training, there are two skills that must be understood and differentiated:

- **Technical Skills** typically refer to skills related to specific technologies, equipment, or processes. These skills are often applied in fields such as engineering, manufacturing, IT, and healthcare.
- **Vocational Skills** (often associated with TVET) refer to skills that are directly related to a particular occupation or trade. These skills are practical and hands-on, preparing individuals for specific jobs or careers in fields like plumbing, carpentry, automotive mechanics, and hospitality.

While both technical and vocational skills involve practical training, vocational skills specifically focus on preparing individuals for skilled trades or occupations, often through structured TVET programs. Technical skills may also be acquired through vocational education but can extend to broader technical knowledge applicable in various industries and sectors.

Training plays a vital role in bridging theory and practice, enabling learners to apply academic concepts in real-world scenarios. However, training without a strong theoretical foundation risks becoming overly narrow and task-focused, limiting adaptability in evolving industries. A well-rounded TVET system combines robust theoretical education—to develop critical thinking and problem-solving skills—with practical training to ensure job readiness.

> *"Proper alignment of these elements has the potential to significantly propel a nation's GDP, enhancing ... economic growth."*

For policy makers, it's crucial to understand TVET as a whole before embarking on policy planning. A fragmented approach will lead to inadequate outcomes. The simplified table provided earlier should be viewed holistically. By grasping the interplay between technical education, vocational education, and training, and how these components interact with the supply and demand sides of the equation, policymakers can develop more strategic, effective policies, management strategies, and funding frameworks. Proper alignment of these elements has the potential to significantly propel a nation's GDP, enhancing workforce readiness and economic growth.

In conclusion, TVET is more than just an educational pathway; it is a dynamic ecosystem that requires thoughtful integration to unlock its full potential. The choice of study, whether it leans toward technical, vocational, or a hybrid approach, directly impacts the learner's career trajectory and, ultimately, the nation's economic prosperity.

Note to ponder*:*
*Some people use the term "****TVET Education****" when discussing their arguments. Personally, and Maya agrees, I find this term redundant—****after all, "Education" is already part of the acronym TVET****. While education is certainly central to TVET, the real*

question lies in the balance between its components—technical education, vocational education, and training. The key issue here is determining ***what proportion of education versus training*** *is most effective for different pathways. We will explore this balance shortly.*

1.1 The Silent War

"Academic education, ... was favoured for cultivating thinkers and leaders. Vocational education, by comparison, was seen as a path for those who worked with their hands"

There has long been a silent tension between the Academic and Vocational spheres.

Historically, the academic world has held the upper hand, viewed as the prestigious path reserved for the elite. In contrast, the vocational route, typically accessed through apprenticeships, required a long journey to gain the social recognition of a Master.

Academic education was traditionally seen as the gateway to leadership and intellectual prestige, while vocational education was often viewed as lesser, focused on practical skills and aimed at the working class.

In Europe, this distinction has contributed to the so-called "silent war" between the two systems, rooted in differing societal values and economic demands. Academic education, associated with higher societal status, was favoured for cultivating thinkers and leaders. Vocational education, by comparison, was seen as a path for those who worked with their hands—essential, yet lacking in social prestige. This created a social hierarchy, reinforcing stereotypes about the value of each path. Tensions grew as both systems competed for recognition, funding, and legitimacy, mirroring broader class struggles and economic shifts.

However, these perceptions are slowly evolving. The modern economy's growing need for skilled technical professionals, alongside efforts to elevate the status and quality of vocational education, is gradually shifting societal attitudes. Vocational education is increasingly recognized as a crucial component of economic development, blurring the traditional lines between the two spheres.

We have come up with this simple table for us below:

Factor	Influence on Perception	Historical and Cultural Context
Social Status	Academic education is often associated with higher social status and prestige.	Historically, formal academic education was accessible primarily to the elite, reinforcing its status as a symbol of privilege and intellectual superiority.
Economic Opportunities	Belief that academic education leads to better-paying jobs and career advancement.	With the industrial and post-industrial economic shifts, white-collar jobs requiring academic degrees became associated with economic success and stability.
Cultural Values	Emphasis on theoretical knowledge and intellectual achievement.	Cultural narratives often celebrate the achievements of scientists, scholars, and professionals who pursued extensive academic education, reinforcing its value.
Flexibility and General Skills	Academic pathways are seen as more flexible, providing broad skills applicable to various fields.	The liberal arts tradition values a broad-based education that cultivates critical thinking, creativity, and adaptability, skills deemed essential for leadership and innovation.
Parental and Societal Expectations	Pressure from parents and society to pursue academic degrees as a mark of success.	Education systems and societal norms have historically promoted the idea that academic achievement is the most reliable path to personal development and societal contribution.
Visibility and Understanding	Lack of awareness and understanding of vocational education's benefits and opportunities.	Vocational education and its pathways to success are often less visible in media and society, leading to misconceptions about its value and potential.

1.3 BENICIO, The Master Mason

"...Upon demonstrating sufficient skill through a "masterpiece," they could attain the esteemed title of master...".

Let's begin in Medieval Europe, a place where Vocational Education was practice as part of its culture.

600+ years ago, Europe had already set up a system of Guilds as a response to the need for organization among artisans and merchants. They were formed to protect economic interests, regulate trade, ensure quality control, and provide a structured system for training new practitioners.

During this time, the path from apprentice to master within the guild system was a rigorous journey of skill acquisition and mastery. Young apprentices, often starting in their early teens, were mentored by masters in their craft, gradually progressing through practical training and complex projects. Upon demonstrating sufficient skill through a "masterpiece," they could attain the esteemed title of master, a status that allowed them to take on apprentices and run their own workshops. This historical model echoes in modern vocational training, where structured progression through certification mirrors these medieval practices.

As an example, we have **Benicio**, a young enthusiast eager to carve his niche as a Master Mason. His journey begins with the basic techniques of stone masonry, under the watchful guidance of seasoned masters, setting the foundation for a career built on precision and creativity in one of the most respected crafts of his time.

This would be Benicio's journey from a young apprentice to a Master Mason during Medieval Europe, including earnings and examples of work at each stage:

MAYA@ ChatGPT

Stage	Age	Description	Duration	Earnings	Example of Work
Apprentice	12-15	Begins under a Master Mason, learning fundamental skills like stone cutting and basic masonry.	5-7 years	Minimal or no wages (stipend)	Assists in stone preparation and simple masonry tasks.
Journeyman	20+	Works for wages, refines skills, learns advanced techniques, and travels to work under different masters.	5-10 years	Regular wages	Constructs complex architectural features, e.g., arches.
Master Mason	30+	Achieves mastery after creating a "masterpiece" to gain guild approval, then leads major projects.	Lifetime	High earnings	Designs and supervises construction of significant structures like cathedrals.

TVET 360

Note to Ponder:

Eastern world also had similar systems to the guild-based vocational training seen in Medieval Europe, though the structures and cultural contexts varied. Many parts of Asia, particularly in China, India, and Japan, had longstanding traditions of apprenticeships and mastery within specific trades or crafts, often integrated into social hierarchies and cultural practices.

However, its differences are as follows:

- *Social structures: In many Eastern cultures, vocational roles were more intertwined with social hierarchies like the caste system in India or Confucian values in China, whereas European guilds were more focused on regulating trade and craftsmanship.*

- *Family-based training: In places like India and China, vocational skills were often passed down within families, making the apprentice-master relationship sometimes familial, unlike Europe, where guilds could regulate these relationships more broadly.*

Hence the question is, why is the European model more dominant as compared to its Eastern counterpart?

1.3 Are Engineers TVET?

The question itself may be flawed, but it's one that is frequently asked.

Let's clarify: The educational pathway for engineers is not part of TVET, but the pathway for engineering technicians is.

> *"...TVET programs do provide technical training relevant to engineering fields ..., these roles support engineers rather than replace them."*

Technical and Vocational Education and Training (TVET) focuses on preparing individuals for specific vocational roles, providing them with the practical, hands-on skills necessary for direct entry into the workforce. Jobs such as automotive technicians, welders, and machine operators typically fall under this category and often require formal qualifications, such as diplomas or certificates.

In contrast, non-TVET professions—like those in law, medicine, and professional engineering—demand a broader academic background, often culminating in higher education degrees. These fields rely heavily on deep theoretical knowledge, extensive academic study, and, in many cases, professional licensure for advancement.

Professional engineers are typically classified as non-TVET due to the significant academic education required. Engineers earn bachelor's, master's, or doctoral degrees from accredited universities and specialize in areas like mechanical, electrical, civil, or chemical engineering. Their training focuses heavily on theoretical knowledge, advanced mathematics, design principles, and complex problem-solving, all of which are critical to the profession. Additionally, engineers often must obtain licensure, which denotes a high level of professional expertise and adherence to ethical standards.

While TVET programs do provide technical training relevant to engineering fields (such as in drafting technology or electronics), these roles support engineers rather than replace them. Technicians, trained through TVET, play vital roles in applying technical knowledge, but professional engineers require a more extensive educational background to design, analyze, and lead projects.

MAYA@ ChatGPT

Profession Type	Examples	Key Characteristics
TVET Professions	- AI Technician - Electrician - Culinary Chef - Welder - Plumber - Graphic Designer - Network Technician - Pharmacy Technician - Medical Laboratory Technician	- Focus on practical skills and specific vocational training. - Direct entry into the workforce. - Often requires apprenticeships, hands-on workshops, and real-world practice. - Qualifications include diplomas, certificates, and sometimes degrees in vocational areas.
Non-TVET Professions	- Lawyer - Physician - Economist - Software Engineer - Psychologist - Architect - Engineers - Chemist -Astronomer - Literature Professor	- Requires broad academic education, often at the university level. - Grounded in theoretical knowledge, research, and analysis. - Professional fields may require further study for specialization - Qualifications typically include bachelor's, master's, or doctoral degrees.

TVET 360

Now that we have familiarized ourselves with what constitutes a TVET job, let's look at how these jobs fall within the 4-Quadrant Matrix that illustrates TVET job types based on the intersection of *Vocational and Technical Skills* with *Traditional and Advanced TVET* levels. It highlights the different job roles, helping stakeholders understand the skill requirements and educational focus for each profession, ensuring that TVET programs align with specific job expectations.

You'll notice that Engineers are absent from this table, and instead, the job title *Technologists* is used. In simple terms, Technologists serve as the bridge between design and practical implementation. They take the concepts created by engineers and bring them to life in real-world applications. More details on their role will be covered in future sections.

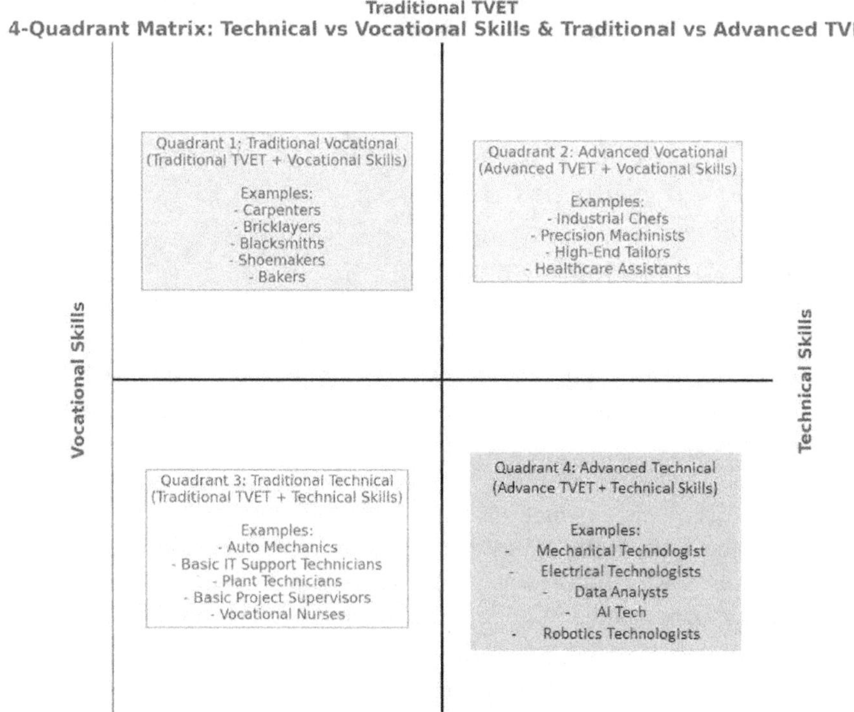

1.4 The Two Towers

"Each system has its unique teaching methods, assessment styles, and career pathways..."

The Two Towers of Learning

The term Universities have a familiar and confident ring to it, whereas terms like Polytechnic Universities can be confusing. Probably because, these two towers come from different perspectives.

To grasp the distinctions and parallels between TVET and traditional academic education, it's important to consider their core features. TVET focuses on practical skills and direct job readiness, emphasizing hands-on training and competency-based assessments.

In contrast, traditional academia prioritizes broad theoretical knowledge, with a curriculum rooted in research and analysis, preparing students for a wide range of careers often requiring advanced degrees. Each system has its unique teaching methods, assessment styles, and career pathways tailored to meet different educational and occupational needs.

As far as look and feel is concerned, there used to be a large difference between these two towers. The Universities used to be much more “pleasant” to the eye, however the environment has blurred somewhat, both these towers seem to have converged to a degree. However, their core business still differs predominantly, but both may now lead to a post graduate qualification.

Maya’s input looks at these differences. Her distinction clearly divides the strength of these towers:

MAYA@ ChatGPT

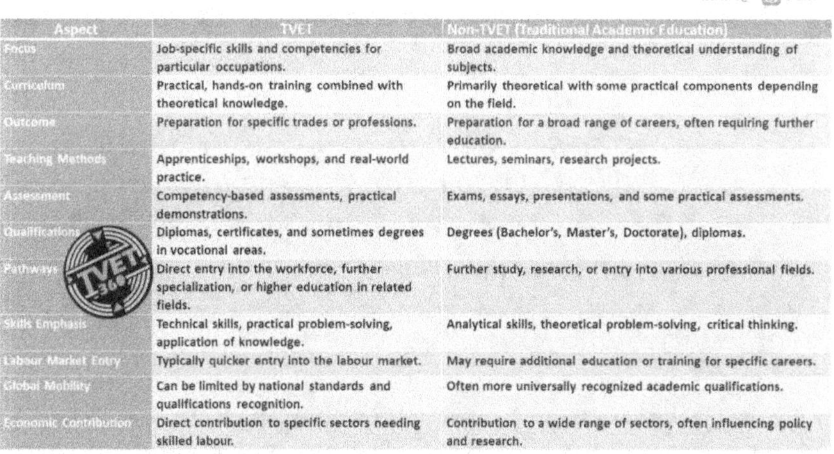

Aspect	TVET	Non-TVET (Traditional Academic Education)
Focus	Job-specific skills and competencies for particular occupations.	Broad academic knowledge and theoretical understanding of subjects.
Curriculum	Practical, hands-on training combined with theoretical knowledge.	Primarily theoretical with some practical components depending on the field.
Outcome	Preparation for specific trades or professions.	Preparation for a broad range of careers, often requiring further education.
Teaching Methods	Apprenticeships, workshops, and real-world practice.	Lectures, seminars, research projects.
Assessment	Competency-based assessments, practical demonstrations.	Exams, essays, presentations, and some practical assessments.
Qualifications	Diplomas, certificates, and sometimes degrees in vocational areas.	Degrees (Bachelor's, Master's, Doctorate), diplomas.
Pathways	Direct entry into the workforce, further specialization, or higher education in related fields.	Further study, research, or entry into various professional fields.
Skills Emphasis	Technical skills, practical problem-solving, application of knowledge.	Analytical skills, theoretical problem-solving, critical thinking.
Labour Market Entry	Typically quicker entry into the labour market.	May require additional education or training for specific careers.
Global Mobility	Can be limited by national standards and qualifications recognition.	Often more universally recognized academic qualifications.
Economic Contribution	Direct contribution to specific sectors needing skilled labour.	Contribution to a wide range of sectors, often influencing policy and research.

1.5 The TVET Family

> *"...they (the family) all share a common goal: to equip learners with the skills necessary for employment and ... the needs of the workforce in various industries."*

The TVET family is International.

Seven siblings, seven names to remember especially if you are going abroad to talk about "TVET". Across the globe, TVET is being called by several other names. Each have a slightly different focus and this makes their objectives different.

These terms reflect regional preferences and slight variations in focus—some emphasize the vocational aspect, others the technical, and yet others the linkage to career pathways. Despite these differences, they all share a common goal: to equip learners with the skills necessary for employment and to meet the needs of the workforce in various industries. Understanding these terms is crucial for global collaboration and knowledge exchange in the field of vocational and technical education.

Below is a detailed table that explains the various terms and acronyms used across the English-speaking world for education focused on preparing learners for the workforce. Each entry highlights the term used, the region or organization that uses it, and a brief description:

Terms for Technical and Vocational Education Across Regions

Term/Acronym	Used By	Description
TVET	UNESCO	Technical and Vocational Education and Training. The comprehensive term used by UNESCO, reflecting a broad approach that includes both education and training aspects to prepare learners for work. Prior to 2001, it was simply "Technical and Vocational Education (TVE)."
VET	European Union	Vocational Education and Training. This term is preferred in European Union documents and discussions, emphasizing the vocational aspect of education and training.
TVSD	Commonwealth of Learning	Technical and Vocational Skills Development. Used by the Commonwealth of Learning and others, this term emphasizes the skills development aspect of vocational education.
FET	UK, South Africa	Further and Technical Education. Often used synonymously with TVET in regions like the UK and South Africa, highlighting the ongoing, advanced nature of technical education.
CTE	USA	Career and Technical Education. Preferred in the United States, this term underscores the career-focused aspect of technical education.
VTE	Less commonly used	Vocational and Technical Education. A less common variant that still appears in various discussions and documents, essentially synonymous with TVET.
PTET	World Federation of Colleges and	From the Global Statement on the Future of Professional Technical Education and Training. This term

	Polytechnics (WFCP)	represents a global perspective on the future direction of technical education and training.

I'm sure there are more than this. This is just a preview, TVET360 will be looking at this in greater detail under the chapter: The TVET Variants.

1.6 TVET – The Big Why?

"Without a strategy, TVET will be another confusing creation we added to our community."

I guess it's time to ask the ultimate question;

- i) **Why is TVET important?**
- ii) **Can the society function without TVET?**

My take - TVET is civilization's tool for turning theoretical knowledge into practical, community-focused action. It takes the abstract understanding from traditional education (read "Tower of Learning") and applies it to meet the immediate and long-term needs of society.

TVET is important to students and youth because it empowers them with practical skills and confidence to pursue careers that are meaningful and fulfilling. It helps young people discover their strengths and talents through hands-on learning, providing them with clear opportunities to build a secure and independent future. By offering a path to self-reliance and professional growth, TVET fosters personal development and instills a sense of purpose, helping students contribute positively to their communities and society.

Without TVET, much of this knowledge would remain theoretical, never fully contributing to real-world challenges or economic progress.

The table below shows TVET's role to the economy and some examples of work.

MAYA© ChatGPT

Aspect of National Economy	Role of TVET	TVET Examples at Work
Addressing Skill Shortages	TVET targets evolving economic needs by training in sectors like technology, healthcare, and green industries, addressing skill shortages.	Training programs in solar panel installation, digital health records management, and advanced manufacturing robotics.
Enhancing Employability	Provides job-specific training that enhances employability, especially for youth, helping reduce unemployment.	Apprenticeships in automotive repair, culinary arts programs, and certification courses in IT support.
Supporting Technological Advancements	Adapts to emerging technologies, preparing a workforce that supports innovation and technological advancements.	Courses in AI and machine learning, biotechnology technician training, and cloud computing certifications.

However, TVET's impact extends beyond just skills training. It fulfills multiple key objectives, including workforce preparation, economic development, and lifelong learning. In the context of economic development—assuming, for a moment, that the nation's economy is all paramount (I hope not)—TVET becomes critical in today's global economy.

By aligning training programs with both current and future labor market demands, TVET helps build a skilled, adaptable workforce that contributes directly to national prosperity and global competitiveness. The keyword here is "aligning"; a TVET system that fails to align with industry needs risks being inefficient or irrelevant.

The crux of the issue is that without a clear strategy, TVET risks becoming a confusing and ineffective part of the educational ecosystem. A well-defined strategy gives TVET a unified purpose, ensuring that it serves not just as a tool, but as a powerful mechanism for societal and economic progress.

Strategy is of upmost importance, for without it TVET is just a tool without a unified purpose. Without a strategy TVET will be another confusing creation we added to our community.

1.7 TVET: The Learning Environment.

"A student's TVET journey doesn't have to be confined to one venue; instead, it can be a blend of all."

Technical and Vocational Education and Training (TVET) provides diverse learning environments tailored to industry-specific needs, focusing on practical skills. It is accessible through various institutions/venues:

1. **Public Institutions**: Community colleges and technical high schools offer foundational and advanced training often at minimal or no cost.
2. **Public/Private Mixed Venues**: These leverage both government support and private investments to enhance specialized training opportunities.
3. **Private Institutions**: Private Trade Schools and Corporate Training Centers (CTC) offer bespoke programs for sectors like hospitality, manufacturing, and business. Training methods vary from traditional classrooms to online and hybrid models, often incorporating real-world applications in workplaces like hotels and factories.

Notably, TVET isn't confined to classrooms or online platforms; much practical training occurs directly at workplaces such as factories and hotels. This on-the-job training under professional guidance effectively links learning to real-world tasks and challenges, making TVET a vital pathway for acquiring industry-specific operational skills.

The table below includes different types of training venues, from more structured educational settings to direct training within the workplace, highlighting the diverse ways TVET can be delivered to meet the specific needs of industries and learners.

Venue Type	Description	Examples	Modes of Learning
Public Institutions	Government-funded schools offering TVET programs at low or no cost.	Community colleges, technical high schools.	Traditional classroom settings, online courses.
Public/Private Mix,	Institutions with both government support and private investments.	Partnership vocational training centres.	Blended learning with in-person and online components.
Note: **Workplace Training (Maybe considered as Mix)**	On-the-job training conducted within companies, such as factories or hotels.	Factory floor training, hotel management training programs.	Direct, hands-on training in a real-world environment.
Private Institutions	Fully privately funded schools offering specialized TVET programs.	Private trade schools, corporate training centres.	Online platforms, tailored corporate training programs.

Although TVET venues—public institutions, public/private partnerships, and private institutions—may seem distinct in their physical presence, they should be seen as interconnected parts of a broader learning ecosystem.

A student's TVET journey doesn't have to be confined to one venue; instead, it can be a blend of all. Public institutions provide accessible foundational knowledge, public/private partnerships offer real-world, industry-focused training, and private institutions deliver specialized expertise.

Together, these venues create a comprehensive learning experience, unified by the philosophy of equipping students with practical, job-ready skills to meet the demands of the workforce. TVET, in this sense, thrives on collaboration across venues, ensuring that learners receive a well-rounded education.

1.8 Greta turns 15!

Happy Birthday Greta!

At what age can an individual begin their TVET journey?

The typical starting age for Technical and Vocational Education and Training (TVET) varies globally, generally commencing after the completion of compulsory lower secondary education. This starting point, usually around 15 to 16 years of age, is strategically chosen to align with the transition phase in a young person's educational journey. This early start is crucial in preparing students to meet the immediate needs of the labour market, enhancing employability, and supporting economic development.

The table below shows the typical age of completion for TVET programs, reflecting when students are generally ready for full employment in different countries:

Country/Region	Typical Starting Age	Age of Completion	Remarks
Germany	16	18-20	Completion usually after dual system apprenticeships.
United States	16-18	18-20	Career and technical education often ends with high school or can extend into community college.
Australia	15-16	18-20	Includes school-based apprenticeships and further training at TAFE institutes.
China	15-16	18-20	Vocational high school or professional college completion.
United Kingdom	16	18-21	Completion of apprenticeships or vocational qualifications at colleges.

As for Greta, she wants to pursue her dream of becoming a pastry baker using a TVET System in Germany, which combines practical, on-the-job training with classroom learning. This is Maya outlining the pathway Greta might follow, including age guidelines for each step:

Step	Description	Age Beginning	Age Completed
Secondary Education	Complete basic education while taking initial culinary courses	15	17
Vocational Training	Enter a dual vocational program specializing in baking and pastries.	18	20
Apprenticeship	Begin an apprenticeship at a bakery to gain hands-on experience.	18	20
Additional Certification	Optional: Pursue further certification in specialty pastries.	21	22

1.9 The TVET Champions!

"These countries exemplify strong policy frameworks coupled with practical implementation strategies..."

The world's best TVET systems, exemplified by countries like Germany, Switzerland, Australia, Singapore, South Korea, the Netherlands, and Canada, stand out not only for their *innovative policies but also for their successful implementation.* These nations:

- Integrate TVET with real-world business needs through strong partnerships between educational institutions and the private sector.
- Emphasize continuous skill development, ensuring their workforce remains competitive in a rapidly changing global economy.
- Maintain high standards of quality and consistency in training across various regions, enhancing national economic competitiveness.

These leaders in TVET highlight the importance of a robust link between vocational education and employment outcomes, driving both individual success and broader economic growth. Keep these champions nations in mind as we will be visiting them and others as and when needed.

The table below lists seven countries renowned for their successful TVET systems, highlighting their innovative policies and effective implementation. These countries exemplify strong policy frameworks coupled with practical implementation strategies that connect TVET with labour market needs, enhancing both employability and economic competitiveness:

Country	Innovative Policy	Examples of Successful Implementation
Germany	Dual System	Combines apprenticeships in companies with vocational schooling; highly effective in preparing skilled workforce.
Switzerland	Strong Public-Private Partnerships	Similar to Germany, integrates educational institutions with private sector needs effectively.
Australia	National Training Packages	Standardized training descriptions that ensure consistency and quality across TVET providers.
Singapore	SkillsFuture Initiative	Focuses on continuous learning, provides resources for all citizens to develop and deepen skills.
South Korea	HRD Korea	Government-led HR development aimed at continuously updating the workforce's skills to meet market demands.
Netherlands	Competence-based Learning	Focuses on practical skills and real-work situations in their TVET curriculum to better prepare students for work.
Canada	Red Seal Program	Ensures that skilled trades standards are uniform across provinces, facilitating labor mobility and recognition.

1.10 Chapter 1.0 Take-Away

Your Take-Away is Ready!

The TVET World provides a comprehensive understanding of the TVET ecosystem, emphasizing its importance in today's global economy. TVET, which stands for Technical and Vocational Education and Training, integrates three core components: technical education, vocational education, and training, all designed to prepare learners for immediate employability in various industries. The chapter highlights that TVET is not just about acquiring skills; it's a learning pathway that equips individuals with both practical and theoretical knowledge, necessary for adapting to evolving industry demands.

The chapter also distinguishes between technical and vocational education. Technical education focuses on higher-level, non-routine roles like engineering, while vocational education trains learners for routine tasks in specific trades, such as carpentry or plumbing. The chapter stresses that policymakers must understand TVET holistically to ensure successful policy planning, as fragmented approaches can lead to ineffective outcomes.

In addition, the historical model of guild-based vocational training in Medieval Europe mirrors today's TVET systems, which emphasize structured progression from apprentice to master. Moreover, the ongoing "silent war" between academic and vocational spheres is discussed, noting a shift in modern perceptions, where vocational training is gaining recognition for its critical role in economic development.

Policy makers and strategists can take away from this chapter the importance of viewing TVET holistically, recognizing the need for a balanced approach between technical and vocational education. Effective policies should avoid fragmentation and instead focus on creating a comprehensive pathway for learners, ensuring that training equips individuals with both practical skills and theoretical knowledge.

Strategists should also appreciate the historical lessons from systems like the European guild model, where structured progression led to mastery, and apply these principles to modern TVET systems. The chapter also highlights the need to elevate the status of vocational education to meet the demands of the modern economy.

Lastly, here are 5 major conclusions:

- TVET goes beyond hands-on skills; it's a complete learning pathway.
- Effective TVET systems require holistic and integrated policy planning.
- Technical and vocational education fulfil distinct workforce roles.
- Guild systems influenced the structure of modern TVET models.
- Balancing theory and practice is key to economic development.

The TVET ORIGINS

Chapter 2: The TVET Origins

The Origins of TVET delves into the historical foundations of Technical and Vocational Education and Training (TVET), tracing its evolution from medieval guilds to modern institutions. We will explore how guilds, the primary entities for regulating trades and ensuring quality during the medieval period, laid the groundwork for structured vocational training. The chapter will also examine the role of mercantilism, the prevailing economic philosophy that influenced the development of vocational education by emphasizing the importance of a skilled workforce to compete in global trade.

Furthermore, we will discuss the transition to the Chambers of Commerce, which adapted the guilds' roles to support broader commercial interests and economic development. By understanding these historical underpinnings, this chapter seeks to answer why European countries today are among the best in vocational training, considering whether their historical practices in TVET have contributed to their current success. This historical perspective will provide insights into the lasting impacts of Europe's educational and economic strategies.

Three Questions

Based on the readings of this chapter. These are important questions to prompt critical thinking among policymakers, politicians, and TVET strategists as they plan their local TVET initiatives:

1. **Historical Continuity and Change:** How does the historical development of TVET in your region influence current practices, and what elements from the past should be preserved or changed to meet today's educational and economic needs?
2. **Adaptation of Historical Models:** Given the evolution of TVET from guilds to modern institutions, how can your TVET system integrate the rigorous apprenticeship and

quality control methods from the guild era while adapting to the flexibility and technological demands of the 21st century?

3. **Economic and Cultural Specificity:** How can your TVET programs be tailored to reflect the specific economic and cultural contexts of your region, rather than replicating TVET models from historically dominant nations which might not fit local needs?

2.1: The Roots of TVET

"While vocational training has always been central to skill development, its structure and focus have changed drastically over time."

TVET can be traced back to ancient civilizations, where apprenticeship models were used to pass down skills in trades and crafts from one generation to the next.

This educational approach has evolved through various stages of human civilization, adapting to the needs of different epochs while retaining its core objective: to equip individuals with the practical skills necessary for employment and entrepreneurship. From the ancient apprenticeships that conveyed specialized crafts skills in civilizations like Egypt and Greece, through the guild-driven training systems of medieval Europe, to the dawn of formal technical education during the Industrial Revolution, TVET has continuously transformed.

Each phase in its evolution has been influenced by the economic and technological changes of the times, eventually leading to the sophisticated and diverse vocational education systems that today cater to a globalized and rapidly changing job market.

Formalization of these practices varied significantly across cultures and epochs:

- **Ancient Times**: Craftsmen in civilizations like Ancient Egypt and Greece trained apprentices in skills like building, metalwork, and pottery.
- **Middle Ages**: Guild systems in medieval Europe formalized apprenticeships, with strict regulations on training and work quality in various crafts.
- **Industrial Revolution**: The shift to industrialized economies in the 18th and 19th centuries highlighted the need for a more formally educated workforce, leading to the establishment of technical schools and institutes.
- **20th Century**: The rapid technological advancements and changing economic structures led to the expansion and formalization of vocational education globally. National policies and international organizations began emphasizing the importance of TVET in economic development and social inclusion.

While vocational training has always been central to skill development, its structure and focus have changed drastically over time. Ancient and medieval apprenticeships were informal, often tied to familial or guild systems. However, the Industrial Revolution and the 20th century introduced formalized institutions and national policies to meet the growing demand for a technologically advanced workforce. Today's TVET systems are shaped by global economic needs, emphasizing innovation, social inclusion, and lifelong learning, far beyond traditional craft-based training.

Maya has summarized the evolution of TVET across different historical periods, providing specific examples that illustrate the formalization of these practices in various cultures and epochs. This table outlines how TVET systems adapted and became more structured over time, driven by the changing demands of economic and technological environments in each epoch.

Epoch	Description	Examples
Ancient Times	Craftsmen trained apprentices in essential skills like building, metalwork, and pottery.	- Egyptian pyramid builders - Greek potters and metalworkers
Middle Ages	Guild systems introduced formal apprenticeships with strict regulations on training and work quality.	- Blacksmiths and weavers in Medieval Europe
Industrial Revolution	The shift to industrial economies necessitated a more formally educated workforce, leading to the creation of technical schools.	- Establishment of the École Polytechnique in France (1794) - Mechanics' Institutes in the UK
20th Century	Rapid technological advancements and economic changes led to global expansion and formalization of vocational education.	- The Smith-Hughes Act (1917) in the USA establishing federal funding for vocational education - Formation of UNESCO (1945), promoting international educational standards

2.2 The Hammer, The Market and The Map

"The Hammer, The Market, and The Map collectively shaped the evolution of early TVET."

TVET has evolved significantly from its historical roots, beginning in the Medieval Age and drawing from practices established in medieval guilds, further developed through mercantilism, and expanded during colonial times. The Hammer, The Market, and The Map symbolize how these elements are interconnected:

- **The Hammer (Guilds):**
  - Functioned as the original centres for vocational training, emphasizing the mastery of specific crafts and trades.
  - Managed through structured apprenticeship programs, ensuring the transfer of skills and knowledge to new generations.
  - Maintained strict quality control over production, setting high standards that are analogous to modern certification processes in vocational education.

e.g., Cloth-makers in Flanders and Goldsmiths in Florence

- **The Market (Mercantilism):**
  - Dominated European economic policies from the 16th to the 18th century, focusing on increasing national wealth by regulating trade and protecting domestic industries.
  - Guilds supported mercantilist policies by enhancing the competitiveness of local industries, thus aligning vocational skills with national economic goals.
  - Promoted economic self-sufficiency, which in turn demanded a skilled workforce trained through guild-like institutions.

  e.g., England's Navigation Acts, requiring goods to be carried on English ships

- **The Map (Colonialism):**
  - As European powers established colonies, they introduced guild systems to new territories, spreading European methods of craftsmanship and vocational training.
  - Helped in establishing a controlled economic environment where the colonizing country benefited from the raw materials and finished goods produced using guild-standard skills.
  - Facilitated the global dissemination of vocational practices, influencing education systems in the colonies.

  e.g., British guilds establishing branches in the American colonies to supply goods back to England

The Hammer, The Market, and The Map collectively shaped the evolution of early TVET. Guilds (The Hammer) established vocational training through apprenticeships, passing down skills and maintaining high standards. Under mercantilism (The Market), guild-trained artisans became essential for economic policies focused on national production and trade regulation. Colonialism (The Map) then spread these practices globally, adapting them to new territories. While guilds provided the foundation for vocational training, mercantilism and colonialism integrated these skills into broader economic policies.

The evolution of modern TVET reflects both the contributions and limitations of these historical phases, further influenced by industrialization.

However, the interconnectedness of guilds, mercantilism, and colonialism laid the groundwork for modern TVET by establishing early systems of vocational training and integrating skills into economic policies. However, the transition to contemporary TVET systems was complex, influenced by broader social hierarchies, evolving economic needs, and political forces like industrialization and globalization. For example, during the Industrial Revolution, the need for skilled factory workers led to the formalization of technical schools, transforming traditional guild training into more structured educational systems to meet industrial demands.

2.3 The Guilds of Power

"These organizations set standards for quality, determined prices, and managed training..."

(Past reference – Refer to BENICIO: The Master Mason)

The history of guilds dates back to the medieval period, originating as associations of artisans and merchants who banded together to regulate their crafts, control trade, and protect their economic interests. These organizations set standards for quality, determined prices, and managed training through apprenticeships, playing a crucial role in shaping the economic and social structure of towns and cities across Europe.

In the guild system, there were two main types: Merchant Guilds and Craft Guilds. Merchant Guilds controlled trade and commerce within towns, managing economic policies and market regulations. Craft Guilds, on the other hand, regulated specific trades or crafts, focusing on standards, apprenticeships, and the quality of work. Typically, Merchant Guilds wielded greater power, as they influenced the broader economic activities and held sway over the trade policies that affected entire towns and regions, making them pivotal in mercantilist strategies.

We have done up two tables, depicting a Craft and a Merchant Guild; the first one that outlines three powerful Craft Guilds from historical times and examples of their significant contributions to their respective societies and economies:

Guild	Location	Contribution
Clothworkers' Guild	Flanders	- Dominated the European cloth market by ensuring high-quality woollen products. - Set standards for fabric quality, influencing trade policies and prices.
Goldsmiths' Guild	Florence	- Controlled the quality of precious metals and craftsmanship. - Their hallmarking system guaranteed the purity of gold and silver, a practice that is still used today.
Shipwrights' Guild	England	- Crucial to naval and commercial shipbuilding, supporting England's maritime expansion. - Contributed to technological advancements in ship design and construction.

These guilds exemplified the power and influence that such organizations could wield during their peak. They not only controlled the economic activities within their trades but also played significant roles in shaping the broader economic policies of their regions, often impacting international trade and economic development.

Now a table outlining three historical Merchant Guilds, detailing their functions and providing specific examples of their influence and operations:

Merchant Guild	Function and Influence	Examples of Operations
Hanseatic League	A powerful confederation of merchant guilds and market towns that controlled trade across Northern Europe. Promoted mutual defence and commercial interests.	Controlled trade routes and cities along the Baltic and North Sea, including trading posts in Bruges, London, and Novgorod.
Merchant Adventurers	An English trading company that managed the export of woollen cloth to the continent and imported other goods. Had significant political and economic power.	Held a monopoly on English cloth traded in Antwerp, fostering significant economic ties between England and the Low Countries.
Venetian Merchants' Guild	Governed the trade empire of Venice, which was pivotal in Mediterranean commerce. Controlled the import and export of goods, securing Venice's wealth.	Managed the lucrative spice trade from the East to Europe, establishing Venice as a major commercial hub in the Mediterranean.

2.4 Meet the Baas Family

It's time for a story.

We decided to use a creative approach to best describe how a successful medieval family would make craft a living during this times. Let us introduce The Baas Family of Flanders

"In the bustling heart of medieval Flanders, Arein Bass, a revered master of the Clothworkers' Guild, wove not just fabrics but also his family's destiny. With his three eldest sons, Joris, Matthys, and Willem, Arein embarked on a venture that would stitch their names into the rich tapestry of history.

Arein, known for his unmatched skill in weaving fine woolens, recognized the potential in the burgeoning mercantilist policies of the era. Under his guidance, his family started producing exquisite cloth that was not only sought after in local markets but also across the seas in the new colonies. He taught his sons that quality would be their greatest advocate.

Joris, the eldest, had a keen sense for trade and navigated the complex trade routes to the colonies. He established trade agreements with colonial merchants who were eager for the luxurious textiles that symbolized European sophistication.

Matthys, the middle son, innovated in the dyeing process, introducing vibrant colors that stood out in the colonial markets, making their textiles uniquely desirable. The youngest, Willem, managed the operations at home, ensuring that the quality of every bolt of cloth met their father's exacting standards.

The family's strategic use of colonial markets, backed by mercantilist policies that favored the motherland's products, allowed them to monopolize the textile market in several colonies. As their cloths draped the figures of colonial elites, the profits returned to Flanders, enriching the Bass family."

The Baas family's success illustrates how the interconnected forces of guilds, mercantilism, and colonialism shaped their prosperity and the broader economic landscape.

By mastering their craft through the Clothworkers' Guild, they maintained high standards and embraced innovation, as seen in Matthys' advanced dyeing techniques. Their ability to adapt to mercantilist policies and seize opportunities in colonial markets highlights the importance of strategic foresight and entrepreneurial thinking.

Their story teaches us that success requires a blend of skill, innovation, and the ability to navigate complex economic systems, reflecting the foundations of modern TVET. Through the guild system, the Baas family not only achieved wealth but built a lasting legacy where quality and innovation became their hallmark, establishing themselves as a powerful name during the mercantile and colonial era.

In real time: **Saint-Gobain**

One true example of a company that began similarly to the Baas family is Carondelet, which eventually became part of Saint-Gobain, a multinational corporation. Saint-Gobain traces its origins back to 1665 in France, during the reign of King Louis XIV, when the company was founded to produce mirrors for the Palace of Versailles. It began as a guild-like enterprise, focused on craftsmanship and quality in glass production, and benefitted from mercantilist policies that protected local industries and enhanced their growth.

Saint-Gobain's story mirrors the Baas family in that it was rooted in a craft (glassmaking) and became successful by mastering production through innovation and quality control. Over time, as European economies expanded, Saint-Gobain took advantage of colonial expansion and international markets to grow, much like the Baas family did by seizing opportunities in global trade. Today, Saint-Gobain is one of the world's largest building materials companies, but its roots in traditional craftsmanship and its adaptation to economic and political changes are a perfect example of how companies can evolve from small, guild-like beginnings to global giants.

2.5 The Age of Mercantilism

"Mercantilism significantly influenced the economic landscape by promoting the development of industries that were key to national interests..."

The Age of Mercantilism, spanning from the 16th to the 18th century, was characterized by a European economic policy that prioritized national wealth accumulation through trade balance control. Nations sought to maximize exports and minimize imports through government intervention, imposing tariffs and granting monopolies to protect domestic industries.

From trading sugar to slaves, this era saw the emergence of powerful maritime empires that extended their economic influence through colonization, extracting resources and establishing trade sea routes globally.

Mercantilism significantly influenced the economic landscape by promoting the development of industries that were key to national interests, such as textiles and shipbuilding. This focus on enhancing national economic capabilities necessitated a skilled workforce capable of operating complex machinery and engaging in sophisticated trade activities.

As a result, TVET systems began to evolve, adapting to meet the needs of these expanding industries. Guilds, which had previously dominated trade and craft training, gradually integrated more formal educational structures to train individuals in specific skills aligned with mercantilist objectives, thereby laying the groundwork for modern TVET systems.

Maya via the table below has presented an interesting read between a Mercantile commodity and TVET in those times:

Commodity	Role of TVET (Historical Context)	Examples	Skill Development Methods
Spices	Skills needed in the cultivation, harvesting, and processing of spices were crucial.	Training in agricultural techniques specific to spice plants; methods for drying and curing spices.	Learned through informal apprenticeships and traditional knowledge within growing communities.
Textiles	Crucial in teaching weaving, spinning, dyeing, and textile manufacturing techniques.	Apprenticeships in textile mills; training in weaving silk and cotton; development of dyeing skills.	Formal apprenticeships and guild training were more common in this sector.
Sugar	Essential for developing skills in the operation of sugar processing equipment and cultivation methods.	Training programs for workers on sugar plantations; courses on the mechanical maintenance of mills.	On-the-job training and experience, often under forced labor conditions on plantations.

Tobacco	Training in the cultivation, curing, and processing of tobacco leaves was emphasized.	Vocational courses in tobacco farming practices; techniques for curing and cutting tobacco.	Informal learning and experience, primarily through hands-on practice.
Precious Metals	Skills in mining, metal refining, and metallurgy were taught.	Training in the operation of mining equipment; apprenticeships in smelting and refining processes.	Skills typically acquired through apprenticeships and hands-on training in mining operations.

2.6 Harry Smith and The Industrial Revolution

"This evolution (Industrial Revolution) was pivotal in supporting industrial growth, adapting training methodologies from traditional guild-based training to more formalized industrial education systems..."

Meet Harry Smith, a fictitious character we imagined in trying to relate to a typical scenario of early TVET due to the 1st Industrial Revolution (1st IR).

The Industrial Revolution marked a shift from guild-based craftsmanship to industrialized economies, emphasizing machine-based manufacturing. As a result, TVET evolved to address the need for operating complex machinery and managing industrial processes. This transition from artisan crafts to industrial skills was crucial in supporting the era's technological advancements and economic growth, transforming traditional training into more formalized industrial education systems.

The Industrial Revolution was significantly shaped by historical economic practices, particularly the transition from guilds to industrialized economies. As the world moved into this era, the focus shifted from manual craftsmanship to machine-based manufacturing. TVET had to evolve in response to these changes. The need for specialized skills transitioned from artisan crafts to operating complex machinery and managing industrial production processes. This evolution was pivotal in supporting industrial growth, adapting training methodologies from traditional guild-based training to more formalized industrial education systems, preparing a workforce for the industrial and technological advancements that defined the era.

Harry Smith's story would be as such:

"Smith, a tenacious young man with dreams of becoming an engineer, chose to enhance his skills at the Mechanics Institute in London, a beacon for aspirants in the industrial age. Working as an apprentice by day at a bustling local factory, he spent his evenings immersed in the world of gears and gizmos, attending lectures and practical workshops.

The institute, founded to democratize education in technical fields, offered Harry not just knowledge but also a community of like-minded individuals. Balancing work and study was no small feat. His days began before sunrise, with hours spent handling machinery, which honed his practical skills. By night, under the dim light of gas lamps in the institute's halls, Harry delved into complex mathematical theories and engineering principles.

Each weekend, he dedicated time to personal projects and experiments, applying what he learned to build models that demonstrated his growing expertise. This rigorous routine was exhausting, yet exhilarating for Harry. His determination paid off as he not only mastered his craft but also forged a path towards his dream, each lecture and shift bringing him closer to the world of engineering he aspired to shape."

Maya has proposed a table depicting Smith's possible daily schedule at an Institute like The Mechanics Institute.

Day	Activity	Time	Description
Monday to Friday	Work	7:00 AM - 3:30 PM	Full-time job at a local factory.
	Dinner/Rest	3:30 PM - 6:00 PM	Time to rest and have dinner before evening classes.
	Evening classes at Institute	6:00 PM - 9:00 PM	Attends lectures and practical workshops on engineering topics.
Saturday	Independent Study/Project Work	Variable	Day dedicated to independent study or group projects.
Sunday	Rest/Leisure	All day	Day off for rest and personal activities.

Course Duration: Typically, courses at Mechanics Institutes during the 19th century could last from one to several years, depending on the subject matter and the depth of study.

This table simplifies the daily schedule to reflect a more typical work and study balance without specific details that might not be historically verifiable. It considers the general operating hours of factories during the era and the known format of evening classes that were common in educational institutions designed for working adults.

2.7 Guilds of The Eastern World

> *"Western guilds declined with industrial capitalism's rise, some Eastern guild aspects persisted, reflecting distinct economic, cultural, and historical contexts."*

Guilds were essential organizations formed to safeguard the economic interests of their members, regulate product quality, control competition, and provide mutual aid. They organized crafts and trades, ensured the transmission of knowledge, maintained standards, and enabled members to practice their crafts fairly. However, mass production and broader economic shifts eventually diminished the guild system's relevance.

Evolution in the Eastern World:

- **China:** Known as "hang" or "gongsuo," Chinese guilds facilitated trade, supported networks, and regulated prices and standards, playing a vital role in the economic life of cities during the Ming and Qing dynasties.

- **Turkey**: In the Ottoman Empire, guilds known as "esnaf" were integral to the commercial and social life. These organizations not only regulated crafts and trade but also played a significant role in the cultural and religious aspects of society, often organizing events and providing social welfare to their members. The "esnaf" ensured the quality of goods and services, controlled prices, and maintained ethical standards within their trades, which were crucial for the economic stability of the region during the empire's peak.
- **Adaptation and Continuity:** In the East, guild functions merged with other social and economic organizations, influencing local economies into the modern era under various names and structures.

While Western guilds declined with industrial capitalism's rise, some Eastern guild aspects persisted, reflecting distinct economic, cultural, and historical contexts. Guilds' legacy, especially in apprenticeships and trade regulation, still impacts modern vocational training and professional organization.

Factors Influencing Guild Development:

1. **Pre-Existing Systems:** In some regions, existing social structures (like India's caste system) organized professions, reducing the need for guilds.
2. **Colonial Influence:** Colonialism introduced economic systems that disrupted local trade organization development.
3. **Cultural and Legal Frameworks:** The absence of supportive legal and cultural frameworks limited guild formation in some areas.
4. **Economic Diversification:** Less economic specialization reduced the impetus for guild formation in primarily agricultural economies.
5. **Alternative Organizations:** Other forms of organization in some regions (e.g., communal village structures in Vietnam) fulfilled guild-like roles.

6. **Modern Industrialization:** By industrialization, the relevance of traditional guilds had waned, giving way to labor unions and professional associations.

This summary highlights the historical significance and evolution of guilds, acknowledging their influence on modern vocational structures while considering regional differences and transformations.

To concisely *address the factors influencing the development (or lack thereof)* of guilds across different regions, including the case of Egypt, Maya has come up with a table that will highlight key reasons guild-like organizations did or did not evolve in various parts of the world, including Malaysia/Singapore, India, Vietnam, Africa, and Egypt.

The absence of guilds in certain regions, including Egypt, underscores how economic organization and labour regulation can vary greatly depending on historical, social, and economic contexts. While guilds played a significant role in the development of trade and craftsmanship in some societies, others developed alternative systems and structures to meet similar needs.

Maya has come up with this table to give us a glimpse of how our historical factors might have affected our Guilds development.

Factors Influencing Guild Development

Region	Factors Limiting Guild Development	Explanation
Malaysia/Singapore	Colonial Influence Economic Diversification	Colonial powers controlled trade and resources, limiting local trade organization development. The economy diversified into different areas that did not necessarily support guild formation.

India	Pre-Existing Social Systems Colonial Influence	The caste system organized professions and trades, reducing the need for guilds. British colonial rule disrupted local economic structures, imposing new trade regulations and systems.
Vietnam	Communal Village Structures Cultural Norms	Village-based and family trades, along with communal structures, served similar protective and regulatory roles as guilds in other societies.
Africa	Kinship and Tribal Affiliations Colonial Influence	Kinship and tribal systems regulated trades and crafts. Colonialism introduced new economic systems that did not support the development of indigenous guilds.
Egypt (Historical)	Pre-Existing Social and Economic Structures Lack of Urban Mercantile Culture	Ancient Egypt had a highly centralized economy controlled by the state and religious institutions, focusing on agriculture, construction, and state projects. The absence of a mercantile culture akin to that of medieval European cities may have limited the development of trade-based guilds.

2.8 The 'Death' of the Guilds

"...the Industrial Revolution diminished the guilds' relevance as the primary arbiters of quality and training..."

The rise of the 1st Industrial Revolution marked a pivotal shift in Europe's economic and vocational landscape, leading to the decline of guilds—institutions that had long regulated trades and skilled labor. For centuries, guilds were the backbone of medieval economies, fostering craftsmanship through structured apprenticeship programs.

Their approach shaped early Technical and Vocational Education and Training (TVET) systems by embedding a culture of meticulous skill development. However, mechanized production during the Industrial Revolution diminished the guilds' relevance as the primary arbiters of quality and training, signaling a transformative period in industrial capabilities.

Mercantilism played a crucial role in this transition. As nations embraced policies aimed at maximizing exports and minimizing imports, the focus shifted towards large-scale production methods that could satisfy growing domestic needs and international demands. This economic policy dovetailed with colonialism, which provided the raw materials necessary for industrialization. Colonies became both the sources of these materials and the markets for manufactured goods, further undermining the guilds' local economic dominance.

Guilds, which once ensured quality through rigorous apprenticeship programs and controlled access to trades, could no longer maintain their dominance in the face of mass production. The new industrial economy valued speed, efficiency, and volume, undermining the guilds' role as the primary gatekeepers of trade skills and training. Consequently, many guilds were either dissolved or became marginalized, leading to a significant transformation in the vocational landscape of Europe. As guilds faded, the need for a workforce adept in industrial technologies grew, reshaping TVET to meet these new demands. Training now had to focus on machine operation and maintenance, skills that were necessary for industrial success but not addressed by the traditional guild system.

Thus, "The Death of the Guilds" was not just a cessation of an old order but also a transformation that paved the way for modern vocational education and training, aligning it with the industrial and technological advancements of the era.

A Tale lost in Time:

In the small town of Manchester, 1794, young Thomas Harding sat at his loom, the rhythmic click-clack of the shuttle a familiar sound. He was an apprentice in the Weavers' Guild, following in the footsteps of his father and grandfather, both proud master weavers. For years, the guild had controlled the town's weaving trade, ensuring every bolt of fabric was meticulously crafted by skilled hands.

Thomas had spent years perfecting his craft, learning every knot, pattern, and technique from his father. The guild had promised security—a future where his expertise would be valued, where customers would seek out his hand-woven cloth for its quality. But things were changing, and Thomas could feel it.

Across town, the newly built cotton mill loomed large, its steam-powered machines churning out miles of fabric. Inside, rows of workers, many unskilled, operated the power looms. Thomas's old friend George, who had once been a fellow apprentice, now worked at the mill. He had traded the wooden loom for one made of steel, the apprentice's promise for a weekly wage.

George visited Thomas one evening, shaking his head as he watched Thomas work. "You can weave as much as you want, but the mill... it's faster, cheaper. The merchants don't care about handcraft anymore."

Thomas glanced at his loom, his fingers running along the thread. He felt the weight of centuries of tradition slipping away, the guild's promises crumbling. His father had warned him of this moment, but Thomas had clung to hope. Now, merchants flocked to the mills, and fewer customers sought the guild's handwoven cloth.

That night, Thomas made a choice. He packed away his loom, bidding farewell to the guild's dying world. Tomorrow, he would walk to the mill, not as a master weaver, but as a factory worker, embracing the future his hands could not stop.

2.9 The Chambers of Commerce (CoC)

"...They (CoC) operate at local, national, and international levels, enabling them to facilitate a global network of trade ..."

The evolution of economic organizations from medieval guilds to modern Chambers of Commerce represents a significant transformation in how business interests are organized and advocated. While the guilds of old were localized, trade-specific entities that regulated practices, maintained quality standards, and controlled trade access, today's Chambers of Commerce serve as broader, more inclusive associations that support a wide array of businesses across various sectors and regions.

Chambers of Commerce can be seen as the modern counterparts to guilds in their role of fostering community among businesses. They operate at local, national, and international levels, enabling them to facilitate a global network of trade and business relationships unlike the confined localities of traditional guilds. This global outreach is crucial in today's interconnected market environment.

Moreover, while guilds were deeply involved in regulating their specific crafts or trades, Chambers of Commerce focus on advocacy, aiming to create favorable business conditions through lobbying for pro-business policies at various governmental levels. They also provide diverse support services including training, networking events, and business advice to cater to the modern entrepreneur's varied needs.

Another important feature was the fact that the Chambers of Commerce were founded by merchants, traders, and business owners to advocate for commercial interests. Their focus is broad, including improving trade conditions, lobbying governments, and promoting economic growth across various sectors. They support multiple industries, with an emphasis on international trade, policy, and networking.

In contrast, guilds were created by tradespeople to regulate specific crafts. They oversaw training, enforced quality standards, and protected members' economic interests by controlling entry into their trade. Guilds were more local and specialized, focused on craftsmanship and maintaining trade monopolies.

While both groups supported their members, guilds regulated skilled labor in specific trades, whereas Chambers of Commerce addressed broader merchant and business needs across industries.

The Chambers of Commerce, therefore, while not direct replacements for guilds, represent a modern evolution of the concept—transforming to meet the needs of a dynamic and globalized economy, making them akin to "modern guilds."

Here's a table that outlines the evolution of the Chambers of Commerce (CoC) in Europe, incorporating perspectives from the era of guilds to better illustrate the transition and evolution over time.

This table shows the broad strokes of how Chambers of Commerce evolved in Europe, moving from non-existence in the medieval period, where guilds controlled economic activities, to becoming crucial advocates for business and trade in a globalized economic environment.

The decline of guilds during the Industrial Revolution due to the mechanization and centralization of production paved the way for Chambers of Commerce to rise and adapt to the new industrial and post-industrial landscapes, reflecting the changing needs and scales of business operations:

Era	Guilds	Chambers of Commerce
Medieval Period	- Dominated local economies - Regulated trades and craftsmanship - Controlled entry and training within specific trades	Not yet established
Early Modern Period	- Continued influence in local trade - Faced challenges from emerging market practices and expanding trade networks	- Emergence in Western Europe as trade expanded - Initially formed to support broader commercial interests
Industrial Revolution	- Decline due to industrialization and the rise of factories - Loss of control over production standards and trade practices	- Rapid growth due to need for industrial advocacy - Supported industrial businesses and broader economic policies
20th Century	- Mostly ceremonial or heritage roles - Some revival in craft and artisan movements	- Fully established as key business networks - Influence on national and international economic policies
Contemporary Period	- Niche resurgence in artisan and craft sectors - Focus on heritage and quality	- Global influence, supporting diverse business sectors - Involved in global trade advocacy, digital

		economy, and sustainability efforts

The Rise of the Merchants

The rise of the merchant class is closely tied to the decline of guilds and the emergence of Chambers of Commerce during the Industrial Revolution. As guilds, which focused on regulating specific trades, lost influence, merchants gained prominence through their role in expanding trade networks and organizing commerce.

With growing international trade and market expansion, merchants accumulated wealth and power, forming Chambers of Commerce to advocate for their interests. This marked a shift from a localized, craft-based economy to a globalized, trade-driven system, where merchants became key players in shaping the new economy.

The merchant class was instrumental in the rise of **capitalism** and the development of global trade, fundamentally changing the economic and social landscape of Europe and beyond. The decline of guilds and the rise of merchant influence directly fueled this transformation.

The earliest Chamber of Commerce in England:

Founded in 1773, the **Liverpool Chamber of Commerce** holds the distinction of being the oldest Chamber of Commerce in England. It was initially formed by a group of merchants in response to the need for better regulation and representation of trade in Liverpool, a significant port city at the time.

Although the Chamber ceased operations in 1796, it was revived in 1850 to address the growing needs of the local business community.

Since then, the Liverpool Chamber has continuously evolved, playing a key role in advocating for businesses, supporting growth, and fostering international trade relationships, while helping companies navigate economic challenges.

2.10 TVET and The Colonial Nations

> *"This integration allowed colonial powers to refine TVET systems not only to meet the needs of their local economies but also to exploit the raw materials and labour available in the colonies."*

The historical trajectory of colonial nations in developing Technical and Vocational Education and Training (TVET) systems offers a distinctive perspective on how colonialism provided these countries with certain advantages over non-colonial nations.

Rooted in the guild systems of the medieval world, -- later in the rise of the Merchant class -- colonial powers had access to structured approaches for skill training and quality control, established during a time when guilds regulated almost every aspect of craftsmanship and trade. These frameworks were pivotal as they laid the groundwork for systematic vocational education, which colonial powers exported to their colonies.

Colonialism expanded these practices on a global scale, integrating the resources and economic needs of the colonies into the broader mercantilist policies of the empire. This integration allowed colonial powers to refine TVET systems not only to meet the needs of their local economies but also to exploit the raw materials and labour available in the colonies. Consequently, these nations developed training programs that were both diverse in skill sets and broad in scope, enhancing their industrial capacities at a faster pace than non-colonial nations, which often lacked such extensive international networks and resources.

Furthermore, the economic boost received from colonial enterprises enabled these nations to invest more significantly in refining their educational systems. This economic advantage facilitated continual improvements in TVET, making it more responsive to industrial advancements and technological innovations. Therefore, colonial nations were uniquely positioned to perfect their TVET systems through enriched resources, economic incentives, and a well-established foundation in guild-based training practices, setting a precedent that many non-colonial nations would struggle to match.

The integration of colonial resources, the economic benefits derived from colonial activities, and the foundational guild systems provided these nations with both the means and the infrastructure to advance their educational systems.

These advantages include:

1. **Resource Utilization**: Colonial nations could exploit the raw materials and labour from their colonies, which allowed them to scale industrial activities and necessitated the development of a skilled workforce.
2. **Economic Benefits**: The wealth accumulated from colonial enterprises enabled significant investments in education and training systems, fostering advancements in TVET to support industrial and technological growth.
3. **Established Frameworks**: Having a historical background in guild-based training gave colonial powers a structured approach to vocational education, which they

adapted and expanded in both their home countries and colonies to meet broad economic goals.

However, it's also important to recognize that this advantage came at significant social and economic costs to the colonized regions, often exploiting local populations and resources, which contributed to long-term developmental disparities. This context is crucial for a balanced understanding of how colonial legacies have shaped modern educational and economic landscapes.

Here's a table summarizing the advantages that colonial nations had in developing their TVET systems, with examples illustrating each point:

Advantage	Description	Examples
Resource Utilization	Colonial powers could access and exploit raw materials and labour from their colonies.	British exploitation of Indian cotton and the training of local workers in textile production.
Economic Benefits	Wealth from colonial enterprises allowed for significant investments in education and training systems.	The wealth generated from Caribbean sugar plantations funded educational reforms in Britain.
Established Frameworks	Historical guild systems provided a structured approach to vocational education, adapted for colonial needs.	Dutch guilds' maritime skills were adapted for use in shipbuilding and navigation training in the Dutch East Indies.

2.11 Chapter 2 Take-Away

Your Take-Away is Ready!

Understanding the historical roots of Technical and Vocational Education and Training (TVET) from this chapter offers critical insights for TVET strategists and planners. It is evident that the evolution of TVET, from medieval guilds to modern systems, reflects significant adaptations to economic, technological, and cultural shifts.

Strategists must appreciate that the historical advantages of certain nations—shaped by guilds, mercantilism, and colonial expansions—cannot be replicated exactly due to differing historical paths. Therefore, current TVET frameworks must be adapted to local contexts while maintaining rigorous standards set by past apprenticeships and quality controls.

TVET (Technical and Vocational Education and Training) and Chambers of Commerce (CoC) complement each other by addressing both the supply and demand sides of the labor market. TVET provides hands-on training that equips individuals with industry-relevant skills, ensuring workforce readiness and lifelong learning opportunities. Meanwhile, CoCs focus on business advocacy, pushing for favorable policies and providing networking and support to businesses. By collaborating with TVET institutions, CoCs help align educational programs with industry needs, ensuring graduates enter the workforce with the right qualifications. This creates a cycle where education feeds into employment, and businesses drive the need for updated training. Together, TVET and CoCs foster a skilled workforce and support economic growth, creating a dynamic and adaptable labor market.

For effective strategy development, it's crucial to integrate these historical lessons, ensuring that TVET programs are robust and flexible, aligned with both current industrial demands and technological advancements. This approach helps in crafting strategies that prepare workforces for future challenges, fostering innovation and growth, while being mindful that not all practices from historically advanced nations are directly transferrable to different contexts.

Lastly, here are 5 major conclusions:

- TVET has its origins in ancient apprenticeship systems, where skills were passed down from master to apprentice.
- Guilds were instrumental in shaping early vocational training, regulating trades and ensuring skill development.
- Mercantilism and colonialism facilitated the global spread of TVET practices by promoting the need for skilled labor in expanding trade networks.
- Industrialization transformed TVET from localized, craft-based training into more formal, institutionalized systems to meet the demands of mass production.
- The rise of the merchant class created a continuous demand for skilled TVET workers to support growing industries and trade.

The TVET STEPS

Chapter 3: THE TVET STEPS

We often struggle to explain what TVET truly is to curious individuals. It's easy to categorize it simply as 'skills' or 'hands-on' learning, but this oversimplification doesn't capture the full scope of what TVET entails.

Such a simplistic categorization, if not addressed, can lead to a misguided understanding of TVET, which may result in poorly informed strategic and action plans.

In reality, TVET encompasses a much broader scope—merging practical skills, technical knowledge, and problem-solving abilities, with the aim of preparing individuals for both immediate employment and long-term career development.

To better explain TVET's comprehensive nature, we introduce the TVET STEPS Framework. This structured model provides a clear understanding of the phases that learners go through, highlighting how they progress from foundational skills to advanced expertise and lifelong career adaptability.

Defining TVET Through the TVET STEPS

1) SkillsFirst - Foundational Skills (Step 1):

In the first step, students build the essential skills necessary to enter a specific trade or technical field. This stage combines basic technical competencies with foundational knowledge, such as literacy, numeracy, and problem-solving. These core skills form the groundwork upon which more specialized learning is built, enabling students to either step into entry-level roles or continue to the next stage of education.

2) SkillsFusion - Intermediate Expertise (Step 2):

This step represents the deepening of technical skills and theoretical knowledge. Here, learners refine their abilities through more focused, trade-specific training. They begin to bridge the gap between theory and practice, applying their knowledge in real-world scenarios. This phase emphasizes critical thinking and adaptability, ensuring that learners can tackle more complex tasks in their chosen fields.

3) SkillsForward - Advanced Mastery (Step 3):

Advanced mastery equips individuals with the expertise needed to excel in highly specialized roles or leadership positions. At this level, students enhance not only their technical proficiency but also their problem-solving, innovation, and critical thinking skills. SkillsForward encourages individuals to engage in upskilling and reskilling opportunities, such as post-degree certifications, Master's, or even Ph.D. programs. These advanced education paths are backed by industry demands, ensuring that graduates not only meet current workforce needs but are also prepared to lead in emerging fields. SkillsForward empowers learners to stay relevant and competitive in the ever-changing job market, making this stage a critical component of long-term career growth. This step prepares them for evolving roles in their industries, where they may be required to manage teams, drive innovation, or take on significant responsibilities.

4) SkillsAdapt - Career Adaptation (Step 4):

The final step emphasizes the importance of continuous learning and adaptability. In today's rapidly changing industries, professionals must upskill and adapt throughout their careers. This step ensures that learners are equipped to evolve alongside technological advancements, industry shifts, and changing workforce demands, enabling long-term career sustainability.

The TVET STEPS Framework shows that TVET is not a one-dimensional form of education but rather a continuous learning journey. It begins with foundational skills and progresses through increasingly complex stages, each building on the last. This continuum not only prepares students for immediate roles in the workforce but also empowers them to adapt and grow as their careers advance.

Learning from TVET Champions

Countries recognized as TVET Champions exemplify best practices in implementing TVET. They use structured approaches similar to the TVET STEPS, ensuring learners progress effectively through each phase. By examining how these nations have developed successful TVET systems, we can gain insights into how to improve global TVET initiatives, making them more responsive to the needs of both industry and learners.

The TVET STEPS Framework offers a clear, structured explanation of TVET, revealing its full breadth and depth. Far from being limited to hands-on training, TVET integrates technical expertise, cognitive development, and lifelong learning, ensuring individuals are prepared not just for jobs but for evolving, adaptable careers. By understanding TVET through this framework, we can appreciate its critical role in shaping a skilled and resilient workforce.

Three Questions

Based on the readings of this chapter. These are important questions to prompt critical thinking among policymakers, politicians, and TVET strategists as they plan their local TVET initiatives:

1) **Integration of STEPS:** How can your TVET programs integrate the STEPS (SkillsFirst, SkillsFusion, SkillsForward, SkillsAdapt) to provide a seamless learning experience that caters to varying needs from foundational skills to advanced innovation and adaptability in your region?

2) **Resource Allocation:** Considering the resource intensity of effectively implementing the TVET STEPS, how will you ensure adequate funding, infrastructure, and educator training to support each stage of the learning continuum?
3) **Cultural and Economic Contexts:** How will you adapt the TVET STEPS framework to fit the unique cultural, economic, and educational contexts of your region to avoid a one-size-fits-all approach and ensure relevance and efficacy?

3.1 TVET - Beyond Skills

"Understanding the complexity of TVET requires appreciating the distinction between technical and vocational education, each catering to different aspects of the workforce."

Before we deep dive into The STEPS, it's helpful if we understand the differences between certain concepts with TVET.

Understanding the complexity of TVET requires appreciating the distinction between technical and vocational education, each catering to different aspects of the workforce. While technical education develops broader, more analytical competencies, vocational education hones specific, hands-on skills. This distinction is crucial to grasp the depth and diversity of TVET, as explored in the following discussion.

Technical education provides students with a foundation in theoretical knowledge and applied sciences, preparing them for roles such as engineers, architects, or IT professionals. These professions are mainly non-routine, involving problem-solving, innovation, and critical thinking. Technical education typically leads to degrees or diplomas and involves a mix of classroom learning and practical labs, designed to address complex industry challenges. The career pathways for technical education are broader and may lead to higher roles or further academic opportunities, whereas vocational education is designed for direct entry into the workforce with specialized skills.

Vocational education focuses on training students for specific trades or occupations, with an emphasis on hands-on, practical skills. The tasks learned are mainly routine, such as those required for roles like plumbing, carpentry, or welding. However, certain aspects can involve non-routine problem-solving and customization, particularly as one progresses in their career. Vocational education leads to certificates or diplomas that prepare learners for immediate job entry.

Technical training equips individuals with the practical skills necessary for roles such as technicians, machine operators, or network specialists. The work in these roles is mainly routine, involving the operation, maintenance, or troubleshooting of technical systems. However, the training also covers non-routine problem-solving when issues arise. Technical training typically leads to certifications or diplomas, preparing learners for specific technical roles.

Vocational training prepares learners for trade-specific skills in areas such as automotive repair, electrical work, or culinary arts. The training is mainly routine, focused on performing specific tasks in real-world work environments. However, as learners advance in their careers, they may encounter non-routine tasks that require problem-solving or creative solutions. Vocational training typically leads to trade certifications or licenses for immediate job readiness.

Thus, TVET is more than just training; it's a comprehensive learning pathway that prepares graduates for both immediate employment and long-term career growth by providing them with both the practical skills and the intellectual tools to thrive in a dynamic workforce.

3.2 TVET "STEPS"

"The TVET STEPS, ... offers a tailored learning journey for individuals at various stages of their career development."

The **TVET STEPS** is a comprehensive framework designed to guide stakeholders through the structured progression of vocational and technical education.

This framework, short for **Skills Training and Education Progression Sequence**, breaks down TVET into distinct stages, helping educational providers design targeted training programs that meet evolving industry demands.

By outlining the stages from initial skill acquisition to advanced specialization**,** it provides a clear understanding of TVET's holistic learning journey.

Here is a summary of the STEPS:

- **SkillsFirst** is the starting point, where learners gain basic, hands-on skills.
- **SkillsFusion** blends those skills with theoretical knowledge, giving them a deeper understanding.
- **SkillsForward** is about moving to advanced training and career growth, where research and innovation is important
- **SkillsAdapt** focuses on lifelong learning, ensuring individuals stay up-to-date with new technologies and industry changes.

Each phase—**SkillsFirst**, **SkillsFusion**, **SkillsForward**, and **SkillsAdapt**—builds on the previous one, guiding learners from foundational skills to specialized roles. While early stages focus on practical, job-ready skills, later phases incorporate theoretical knowledge, research, and innovation.

Importantly, learners don't need to complete all steps to succeed. Each stage can independently equip students with the skills they need, offering flexibility based on individual goals and career paths. Some may find early steps sufficient for workforce entry, while others pursue advanced training for continued growth.

For example, **SkillsFusion** blends hands-on skills with deeper theoretical understanding, preparing learners for industry challenges, while **SkillsForward** emphasizes advanced training and research. **SkillsAdapt** ensures ongoing learning, helping individuals stay current with new technologies.

The TVET STEPS

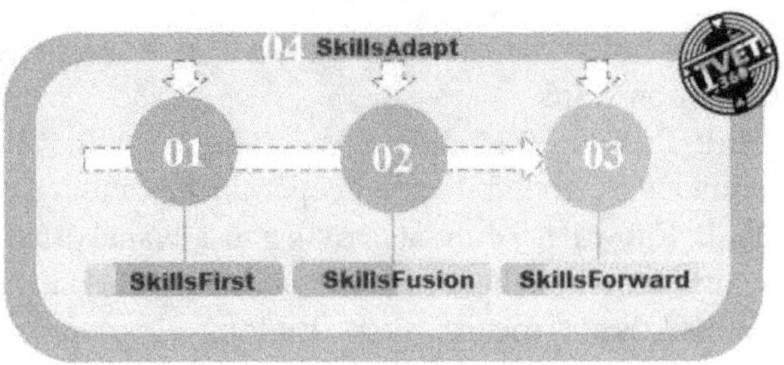

Hence, The TVET STEPS, illustrated above, offers a tailored learning journey for individuals at various stages of their career development. From foundational hands-on skills to advanced research and continuous adaptability, the STEPS ensures learners acquire the necessary competencies to thrive in rapidly changing industries.

How will understanding and applying **The TVET STEPS** benefit all stakeholders?

To summarize, the following table below outlines some of the key uses of **The TVET STEPS** for four types of stakeholders: Learning Institutions, TVET Students, Industries, and Communities.

Stakeholder	Uses of TVET STEPS
Institutions of Learning	1. Provides a **structured framework** to design targeted TVET programs that align with industry standards.
	2. Helps evaluate and **measure student progress and outcomes**, ensuring continuous program improvement.
	3. Ensures a **balance between theoretical knowledge** and practical skills, enhancing curriculum relevance and addressing real-world needs.

TVET Students-to-be	1. Offers **transparent career pathways**, guiding students from basic skills to specialization, helping them better plan their careers.
	2. Shows flexibility, letting students **enter the workforce at different stages** based on their goals, and equips them with options for **continued learning**.
	3. Prepares students for both **immediate employment** and adaptability to new technologies through **lifelong learning** (SkillsAdapt).
Industries	1. Allows **HR departments** to effectively **plan and strategize** workforce development, ensuring the right type of talents are recruited to meet both **current** and **future needs**.
	2. Ensures industries gain a workforce equipped with both **practical skills** and **theoretical knowledge**, alongside the **adaptability** to meet evolving industry demands. This helps industries **address skill gaps** and maintain a **sustainable, future-ready workforce** capable of navigating technological advancements and market changes.
Communities	1. Offers a **big-picture view** of TVET, helping communities understand its comprehensive role in fostering both **technical skills** and **intellectual growth**.
	2. Builds **community awareness** of how TVET contributes to **long-term economic sustainability** and **local development** through skilled workers and adaptable learning.
	3. Helps communities **better understand the various pathways** that TVET provides, promoting **engagement** and **support** for both learners and institutions.

3.3 STEP 01: SkillsFirst

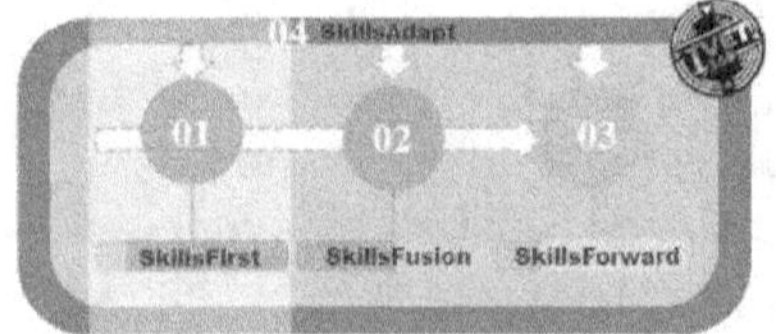

The first continuum point of TVET STEPS is the "SkillsFirst" type programs, operating under the "Pathway - Purely Practical" model, is uniquely tailored for learners who are eager to acquire immediate, hands-on skills for swift entry into the workforce. This program focuses exclusively on practical training, providing an **almost 100% hands-on learning experience**. It is especially beneficial for those who prefer direct engagement and quick application of skills over theoretical study.

With a duration ranging from a few weeks to several months, "SkillsFirst" offers flexibility to accommodate different learning paces and career urgencies. This program is particularly well-suited for fields requiring manual and technical skills, such as carpentry, electrical work, plumbing, and automotive repair. Participants engage in intensive practical sessions where they learn and apply skills in real-world scenarios, enabling them to master essential tasks efficiently.

Ideal for individuals seeking rapid skill development without the commitment to long-term education, "SkillsFirst" ensures that participants are job-ready in a short period. It effectively prepares learners for immediate employment, providing them with the tools and expertise needed to succeed in demanding technical professions.

An Example:

In SkillsFirst for automotive repair, TVET focuses on building foundational, hands-on skills essential for entry-level technicians. The program teaches students the basics of vehicle maintenance, including tools usage, safety practices, and routine services like oil changes, tire rotations, and brake inspections. This stage emphasizes practical experience, allowing learners to develop core competencies needed to work in automotive repair shops, laying the groundwork for more specialized training in future stages.

Students who complete this foundational step can find employment in auto repair shops, service centers, or dealerships, performing basic vehicle maintenance tasks. They may also work in fleet maintenance for companies with vehicle fleets, such as transportation or delivery services. This entry-level role provides the opportunity to gain on-the-job experience, opening pathways for further specialization in advanced automotive repair and diagnostics.

3.4 STEP 02: SkillsFusion

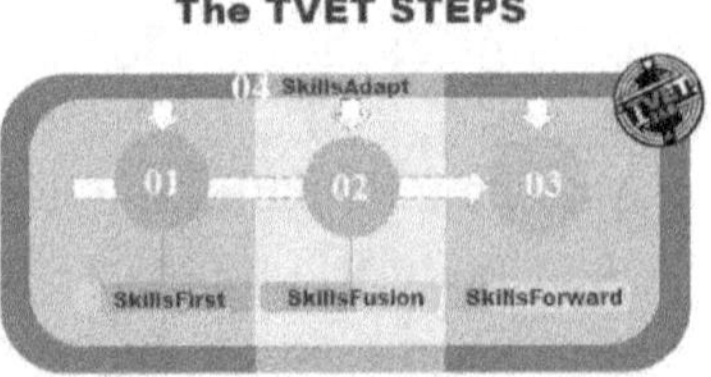

The second continuum point of TVET STEPS is the "SkillsFusion" programs, "Pathway - Balanced Theory and Practice," **effectively combines practical training with theoretical knowledge.** It offers a mix ranging from *50% practical and 50% theoretical to 70% practical and 30%* theoretical content. This balance suits those who seek both a solid understanding and the ability to apply skills in real-world settings.

Spanning six months to four years, the program is adaptable to various professional needs, making it ideal for fields such as healthcare, engineering, IT, and trades. For instance, healthcare students might split their time between classroom learning about medical basics and hands-on clinical experiences. Engineering students could merge theoretical coursework on principles like mechanics with practical labs and projects.

This program targets individuals aiming for a comprehensive educational experience that prepares them for both immediate job entry and future career advancement, offering a strong theoretical base to support practical skills application.

The duration of the program can vary significantly, from six months to four years, accommodating different levels of certification and depth of knowledge required by various professions. This flexible approach makes it suitable for a wide array of career paths, from healthcare and engineering to IT and trade skills.

An Example:

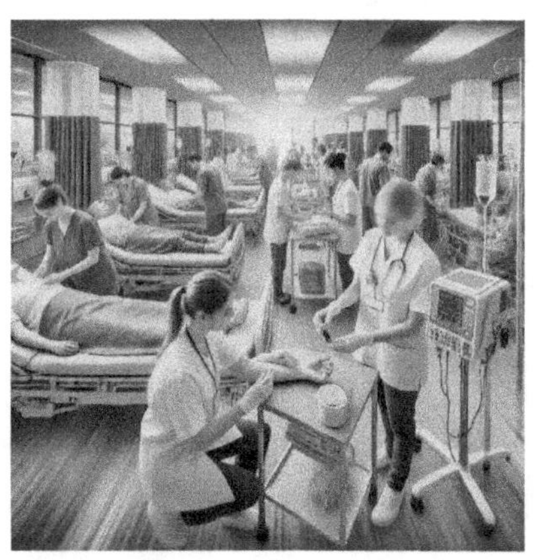

In SkillsFusion for healthcare, TVET blends practical skills with theoretical knowledge to deepen learners' understanding of the field. Students learn essential healthcare practices such as patient care, basic medical procedures, infection control, and the use of medical equipment. This stage emphasizes both hands-on training in simulated environments and classroom learning on topics like anatomy, pharmacology, and medical ethics, ensuring that learners develop a more comprehensive skill set.

Graduates from this stage can work in roles such as nursing assistants, medical technicians, or phlebotomists in hospitals, clinics, or long-term care facilities, with opportunities to pursue further specialization in medical fields.

3.5 STEP 03: SkillsForward

The TVET STEPS

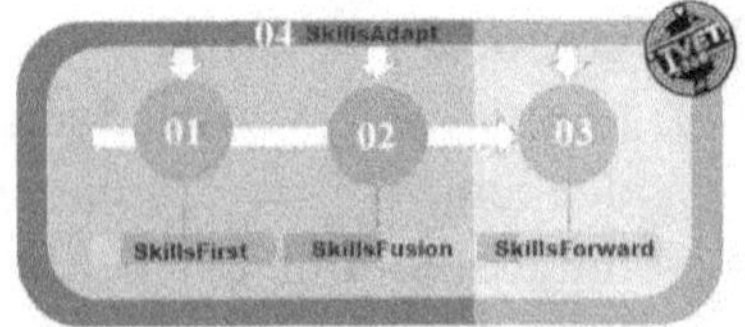

The third continuum point of TVET STEPS is the "SkillsForward" program, titled "Pathway - Advanced Academic and Research," is designed for individuals focused on high-level research, innovation, and academic careers within vocational fields. This pathway emphasizes a research and academic orientation, providing participants with the knowledge and skills necessary to lead in innovation and scholarly pursuits.

Typically extending from four to eight years, including options for an Industry PhD, this program is tailored for deep specialization. It is well-suited for fields where advanced research and development are critical, such as biotechnology, advanced manufacturing, and renewable energy technologies. For example, a participant might engage in extensive research projects in renewable energy, aiming to develop new sustainable technologies, supported by academic coursework that deepens their understanding of energy systems, project management, and innovation strategies.

This pathway attracts those who are not only interested in acquiring advanced technical skills but also in contributing to the scientific community through research publications and technological advancements. It prepares them for roles that require a high degree of expertise and leadership, such as leading R&D departments in corporations or academic positions at universities.

An Example:

In SkillsForward for renewable energy technologies at the PhD level, TVET emphasizes advanced training, research, and innovation in the field. Learners focus on specialized areas such as solar power systems, wind energy, and energy storage technologies, blending theoretical knowledge with cutting-edge research projects to address industry challenges. This stage fosters critical thinking, encouraging learners to develop new technologies, optimize existing systems, and contribute to sustainable energy solutions.

Graduates with a PhD in renewable energy technologies can pursue roles as research scientists, energy consultants, or university professors, working in research institutions, government agencies, or renewable energy companies to lead innovation and policy development in the renewable energy sector.

3.6 STEP 04: SkillsAdapt

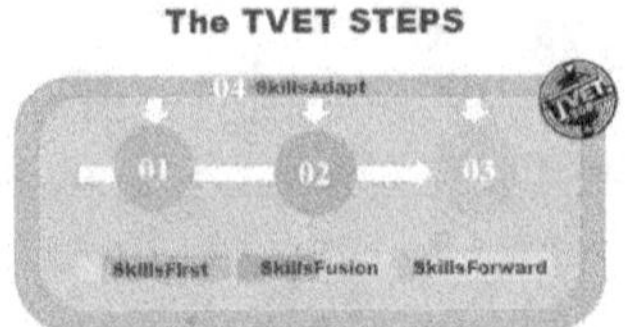

The final continuum point of TVET STEPS is the "SkillsAdapt" program, under the "Pathway - Continuous Learning and Adaptability," caters to TVET professionals at any career stage who need to update their skills or adapt to new technologies and industry demands. This pathway is characterized by its flexible format, which includes a variety of short courses, online modules, and workshops, allowing for tailored learning experiences that meet individual needs and schedules.

The duration of each component within the program varies depending on the specific skill or technology being addressed. For instance, a professional in the automotive industry might take a short course on electric vehicle technology, while a software developer might engage in online modules to learn new programming languages or development frameworks as they emerge.

This pathway is designed for ongoing professional development, making it ideal for those who wish to stay ahead in rapidly changing fields. It supports continuous growth and adaptability, ensuring that professionals can maintain relevance and competitiveness in their careers by quickly integrating new knowledge and skills.

3.7 A Stairway for TVET

The entire stairway was described component by component in the previous chapters -- 3/02-3/05. The TVET STEPS continuum is designed to assist readers in understanding how TVET is being packaged as a learning experience. It is not necessarily a linear progression as depicted by the image, but mostly it does follow such a movement.

The TVET STEPS

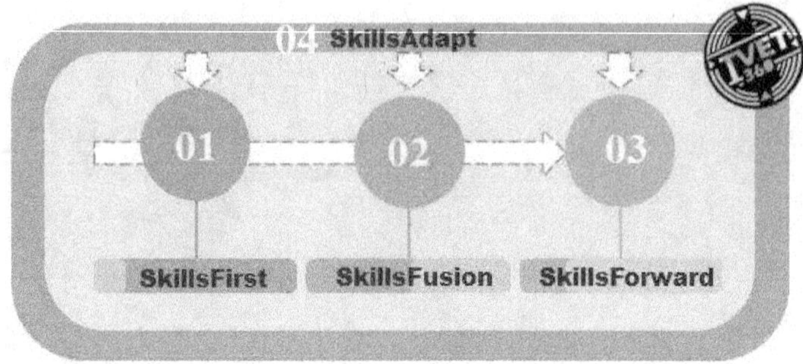

By encompassing four distinct pathways: SkillsFirst, SkillsFusion, SkillsForward, and SkillsAdapt, the STEPS offers a tailored educational journey for individuals at various stages of their career development. From foundational hands-on skills to advanced research and continuous adaptability, the STEPS ensures learners acquire the necessary competencies to thrive in rapidly changing industries. Emphasizing a blend of practical experience and theoretical knowledge, the STEPS prepares individuals for immediate workforce entry, ongoing career advancement, and lifelong learning.

In a nutshell, TVET STEPS is as follows:

- Structured Skill/Academic Progression (Inner Points): The SkillsFirst, SkillsFusion, and SkillsForward stages represent a structured progression from basic skill acquisition to advanced specialization. This pathway ensures learners build a solid foundation, integrate theoretical and practical knowledge, and achieve expertise in their vocational fields.
- Continuous Learning and Adaptability (Outer Point): The SkillsAdapt stage, conceptualized as the outer layer of the bullseye, underscores the necessity of ongoing learning and the ability to adapt to new challenges. It highlights that vocational education does not end with formal training but is a lifelong process that extends beyond initial employment and specialization.

TVET360 has designed a table that again captures the discussion above. This table reflects the structure of the STEPS, detailing each pathway's program name, learning experience, ideal audience, and duration of study, now including SkillsAdapt with its focus on continuous learning and adaptability across various career stages:

MAYA@ ChatGPT

Continuum Point	Program Name	Learning Experience	Ideal For	Duration
SkillsFirst	Pathway - Purely Practical	100% Hands-On	Learners seeking immediate hands-on skill acquisition for quick entry into the workforce.	Weeks to months
SkillsFusion	Pathway - Balanced Theory and Practice	50% Practical 50% Theory to 70% Practical 30% Theory	Those looking for a flexible blend of practical skills and theoretical knowledge.	6 months to 4 years
SkillsForward	Pathway - Advanced Academic and Research	Research and academic focus	Individuals aiming for high-level research, innovation, and academic careers within vocational fields.	4 to 8 years (including Industry PhDs)
SkillsAdapt	Pathway - Continuous Learning and Adaptability	Varies; includes short courses, online modules, workshops, etc.	Professionals at any career stage needing to update skills or adapt to new technologies and industry demands.	Varies; dependent on the specific skill or technology

Conclusion:

As discussed before, there has often been a tendency to define TVET narrowly, focusing primarily on its hands-on, skills-based aspects. However, this approach overlooks the multidimensional nature of TVET, which integrates practical skills with theoretical knowledge, research, and adaptability. The TVET STEPS framework helps refine this definition, presenting TVET as a continuum rather than a single step. By understanding TVET as a progression of learning stages, stakeholders can better plan and implement strategies that address both current and future workforce needs, while gaining a more complete understanding of the true essence of TVET.

For planners and policymakers, the TVET STEPS provides an invaluable tool for strategic planning. Understanding the progression from basic skill acquisition to advanced research and continuous learning helps in designing programs that cater to various career stages and industry needs. By identifying which STEPS are most relevant to different sectors—whether it's a SkillsFirst program for immediate workforce readiness or a SkillsForward initiative for specialized industries—planners can align educational outcomes with specific labor market demands."

Additionally, the emphasis on SkillsAdapt ensures that professionals are not only trained for their current roles but are prepared to stay competitive and relevant in evolving industries. This component underscores the importance of lifelong learning in today's rapidly changing work environments, allowing TVET systems to remain flexible and responsive to technological advances and market shifts.

In conclusion, the TVET STEPS framework offers a structured yet adaptable approach that not only supports individual career growth but also empowers policymakers and planners to develop targeted, forward-thinking initiatives. By using this framework, stakeholders can make more informed decisions that are aligned with both immediate workforce needs and the long-term demands of a rapidly evolving global economy.

3.8 A Rubric for TVET STEPS

Ever wondered how Great Britain, China, or Singapore structure their TVET systems across the TVET STEPS framework?

How do their approaches to vocational education compare?

Our next aim with the TVET STEPS is actually to evaluate selected nations and see how their TVET Learning Experience is stacked up. Hence, in in attempting to do so, we need to create an evaluative tool to enable us to proceed. TVET360 has designed a simple tailored tool specifically for assessing nations based on the TVET STEPS (SkillsFirst, SkillsFusion, SkillsForward, SkillsAdapt). This rubric evaluates how effectively each country implements its TVET strategy across these stages:

MAYA@ ChatGPT

Rating	Criteria for SkillsFirst Pathway	Criteria for SkillsFusion Pathway	Criteria for SkillsForward Pathway	Criteria for SkillsAdapt Pathway
Weak	Offers minimal practical training with limited scope and poor industry alignment.	Theoretical and practical training are disjointed with scarce real-world application.	Little focus on innovation; lacks industry PhDs and advanced training initiatives.	Inadequate support for ongoing learning; limited upskilling and reskilling opportunities.
Medium	Provides basic hands-on training with some industry connection.	Integrates theoretical education with practical training to a moderate extent.	Some initiatives for innovation but limited in scope or impact.	Offers some lifelong learning opportunities but with limited scope or effectiveness.
Strong	Comprehensive hands-on training well aligned with industry needs.	Effective integration of theoretical and practical training with good industry relevance.	Strong focus on innovation with some industry PhDs and advanced training.	Robust support for lifelong learning with effective upskilling and reskilling programs.
Very Strong	Exceptional hands-on training with deep industry integration and high effectiveness.	Seamless and highly effective integration of theory and practice with strong industry partnerships.	Pioneering innovation with extensive mature industry PhDs and cutting-edge training programs.	Comprehensive and highly effective lifelong learning systems, with extensive upskilling and reskilling.

This *rubric allows for a detailed and structured evaluation of how nations implement their TVET strategies, ensuring that each stage is assessed based on its development and integration with industry requirements, focus on innovation, and support for lifelong learning.

Let's begin!

Important:** *TVET360 also likes to stress that,* ***The TVET STEPS *and* ***TVET STEPS Rubrics*** *frameworks provide structured and comprehensive methods for evaluating and enhancing Technical and Vocational Education and Training (TVET) across nations. While they offer clear guidelines and emphasize crucial aspects such as industry alignment and innovation, their effectiveness may vary due to cultural, economic, and resource disparities among countries. These tools should be adapted to local contexts and used alongside qualitative assessments and feedback mechanisms to ensure relevance and effectiveness in diverse global settings.*

3.9 TVET STEPS and The European Nations

MAYA© ChatGPT

TVET STEPS	General Description of European Nations' Strategy	Rating
SkillsFirst	European nations generally invest heavily in vocational training, with Germany at the forefront, offering a highly structured and industry-aligned system. Other nations like the UK and France also have strong programs, though Spain and Poland are somewhat inconsistent.	Strong
SkillsFusion	There is a strong emphasis on integrating theoretical and practical training, particularly effective in Germany and France. The UK and Poland show good integration, while Spain faces more challenges in consistency.	Strong
SkillsForward	Innovation varies significantly, with Germany leading in integrating cutting-edge technologies and methods. The UK and France also focus on innovation but to a lesser extent, while Spain and Poland are still developing their capabilities in this area.	Medium
SkillsAdapt	Lifelong learning initiatives are widespread, especially in Germany and France, with strong governmental support. The UK and Poland are progressing, whereas Spain has more limited success in fully implementing these programs.	Medium

Summary:

This table offers a general overview across typical European nations' TVET strategies:

- **SkillsFirst** and **SkillsFusion** are generally strong across Europe, with well-established vocational training systems that integrate practical and theoretical training effectively.

- **SkillsForward** and **SkillsAdapt** show more variation, with Germany typically excelling in innovation and lifelong learning initiatives. Other nations like Spain and Poland are still enhancing these aspects of their TVET systems.

To have a better look at how some nations fare within these region, let view several cases form this region.

CASE #1: GERMANY

Germany's TVET strategy across the TVET STEPS:

MAYA@ ChatGPT

TVET STEPS	Description of Germany's Strategy	Rating
SkillsFirst	Germany provides exceptional hands-on vocational training, deeply integrated with industry needs, and is recognized globally.	Very Strong
SkillsFusion	The dual education system effectively combines theoretical learning with practical training in a real-world environment.	Very Strong
SkillsForward	Germany is a leader in innovation with extensive collaborations between universities and industries, including numerous industry PhDs.	Very Strong
SkillsAdapt	Lifelong learning is a key component of the German education system, with widespread and effective programs for upskilling and reskilling.	Very Strong

Explanation:

- **SkillsFirst**: Germany's vocational training system is renowned for its excellence and the deep integration of training with industry demands, fitting the criteria for a "Very Strong" rating perfectly.
- **SkillsFusion**: The German dual education system is exemplary, allowing students to split their time between an educational institution and working as a trainee in a company, thus gaining both theoretical knowledge and practical experience highly relevant to their field of study.
- **SkillsForward**: Innovation is a hallmark of German TVET, with strong government and industry support for research and development. This includes well-established industry PhD programs that contribute significantly to both academic and industrial sectors.
- **SkillsAdapt**: Germany emphasizes lifelong learning with robust continuing education and professional development programs that are accessible and effective, ensuring ongoing workforce competitiveness and adaptability.

Germany's approach to TVET represents a comprehensive and effective model, meeting the highest standards across all stages of the TVETSTEPS R rubric, which justifies the "Very Strong" ratings across the board.

CASE#2: FINLAND

Finland's TVET strategy across the TVET STEPS:

MAYA© ChatGPT

TVET STEPS	Finland Description and Explanation	Rating
SkillsFirst	Finland emphasizes robust initial vocational training that focuses on practical skills in various industries.	Strong
SkillsFusion	Integrates theoretical and advanced technical training, tailored to meet both local and international industry standards.	Strong
SkillsForward	Encourages innovation through R&D and collaboration between educational institutions and industries, particularly in technology-driven sectors.	Very Strong
SkillsAdapt	Promotes lifelong learning with continuous education opportunities, helping professionals adapt to new technologies and market demands.	Strong

Finland's TVET strategy is marked by a well-rounded and effective approach, strongly supporting vocational training from the foundational level to continuous professional development and innovation. The integration of vocational training with industry needs and the focus on lifelong learning are key strengths of the Finnish system.

<u>CASE#3: UNITED KINGDOM</u>

UK's TVET strategy across the TVET STEPS:

TVET STEPS	UK Description and Explanation	Rating
SkillsFirst	Provides foundational skills through vocational qualifications at levels 1 to 8, fostering practical learning from an early age.	Strong
SkillsFusion	Offers advanced apprenticeships and vocational qualifications that combine technical skills training with critical thinking and managerial skills.	Strong
SkillsForward	Encourages continuous professional development and innovation through higher vocational qualifications up to master's level in technical fields.	Very Strong
SkillsAdapt	Supports lifelong learning with flexible adult learning programmes and retraining options, adapting to the needs of an aging workforce and technological advancements.	Strong

The UK's TVET strategy is robust, with a strong emphasis on both foundational learning and advanced skills development, fostering innovation and adapting to changing industry and societal needs effectively.

3.10 TVET STEPS and The Asian Nations

TVET STEPS	General Description of Asian Nations' Strategy	Rating
SkillsFirst	Many Asian countries invest significantly in vocational training, with advanced systems in nations like Japan and South Korea, though quality can vary in larger and less developed nations like India and Indonesia.	Medium
SkillsFusion	Integration of theoretical and practical training is emphasized, particularly strong in technologically advanced countries, but hindered by resource constraints in less developed areas.	Medium
SkillsForward	There are pockets of innovation, especially in countries with better resources and governmental support, but widespread, effective implementation across all nations is limited.	Medium
SkillsAdapt	Initiatives for lifelong learning and skills development are in place, with varying degrees of success and implementation challenges across the region.	Medium

Summary:

This table provides a generalized view across the typical Asian nations' TVET strategies. The ratings reflect an overall "Medium" level due to the diversity in economic development, resources, and governmental support which results in varied effectiveness and implementation of TVET strategies across the continent.

To have a better look at how some nations fare within these region, let view several cases form this region.

<u>CASE #1: JAPAN</u>

Japan: TVET strategy across the TVET STEPS:

MAYA@ ChatGPT

TVET STEPS	Description of Japan's Strategy	Rating
SkillsFirst	Japan provides extensive, high-quality vocational training in various sectors, well-integrated with industry needs and technology.	Very Strong
SkillsFusion	Japan excels in integrating theoretical education with practical training, supported by a strong tradition of craftsmanship and technology.	Very Strong
SkillsForward	Japan is a global leader in innovation, with a focus on continuous improvement and technological advancement in its vocational training.	Very Strong
SkillsAdapt	There are numerous initiatives for lifelong learning, supported by government and industries, although participation rates can be improved.	Strong

Explanation:

- **SkillsFirst**: Japan's vocational training is notable for its rigor and alignment with technological advancements and industry requirements, meriting a "Very Strong" rating.
- **SkillsFusion**: The integration of theory and practice is deeply embedded in Japan's educational philosophy, particularly through the system of "Kosen" (Colleges of

Technology), which combines high-level engineering education with practical skills training.

- **SkillsForward**: Innovation is central to Japan's approach to TVET, particularly in fields like robotics, automotive engineering, and electronics, making it a leader in incorporating cutting-edge technology into vocational training.
- **SkillsAdapt**: While Japan has robust programs for lifelong learning and skills development, there are opportunities to increase engagement and participation across a broader segment of the population.

Overall, Japan's TVET system is one of the most advanced and well-integrated globally, reflecting the country's commitment to maintaining a highly skilled workforce. The slight caveat in the "SkillsAdapt" area points to the potential for even greater emphasis on encouraging broader participation in ongoing education and training programs.

CASE #2: SOUTH KOREA

South Korea's TVET strategy across the TVET STEPS:

MAYA@ ChatGPT

TVET STEPS	Description of South Korea's Strategy	Rating
SkillsFirst	South Korea offers high-quality vocational training, heavily supported by both government and industry, especially in sectors like electronics and automotive.	Very Strong
SkillsFusion	The integration of theoretical and practical training is exemplary, facilitated by a strong educational system and significant investments in training facilities.	Very Strong
SkillsForward	South Korea is a leader in innovation within TVET, continuously incorporating new technologies and methodologies in training programs.	Very Strong
SkillsAdapt	There are comprehensive initiatives for lifelong learning and skills development, but there is room for improvement in accessibility and participation.	Strong

Explanation:

- **SkillsFirst**: South Korea's vocational training is notably advanced, with substantial government and corporate investment ensuring that training programs are closely aligned with industry needs and technological advancements, earning a "Very Strong" rating.
- **SkillsFusion**: The country's educational policies successfully blend theoretical knowledge with practical skills, supported by world-class training facilities and a curriculum that meets the high demands of its industrial sectors.
- **SkillsForward**: Innovation is a hallmark of the South Korean approach to TVET, with ongoing efforts to integrate cutting-edge technology and foster a culture of continuous improvement in vocational education.
- **SkillsAdapt**: While South Korea has a solid framework for promoting lifelong learning and professional development, enhancing the reach and engagement of these programs could further improve their effectiveness.

Overall, South Korea's TVET system ranks among the best globally, reflecting the country's commitment to maintaining a competitive edge by investing in a highly skilled workforce. The system's slight limitations in "SkillsAdapt" highlight areas where there could be more focus on ensuring that lifelong learning opportunities are accessible and appealing to all segments of the population.

CASE#3: SINGAPORE

Singapore's TVET strategy across the TVET STEPS:

MAYA@ ChatGPT

TVET STEPS	SINGAPORE-Description and Explanation	Rating
SkillsFirst	Singapore provides robust initial vocational training through institutions like the Institute of Technical Education (ITE), focusing on essential skills for sectors such as electronics, hospitality, and healthcare.	Very Strong
SkillsFusion	There is a significant emphasis on blending advanced technical skills with soft skills through Polytechnics, enhancing students' readiness for diverse career paths.	Very Strong
SkillsForward	Encourages innovation through strong links with industry and research, integrating advanced technical education with emerging fields like biotechnology and fintech.	Very Strong
SkillsAdapt	Offers continuous upskilling and reskilling opportunities, supported by initiatives like SkillsFuture, which focuses on lifelong learning and adaptation to new technologies.	Very Strong

Singapore's TVET strategy is exemplary, characterized by a comprehensive and forward-thinking approach that not only prepares students for immediate employment but also ensures continual growth and adaptability in a rapidly changing global job market. The nation's investment in both foundational and advanced training, coupled with strong government support for lifelong learning, sets a high standard for TVET systems worldwide.

<u>CASE#4: CHINA</u>

China's TVET strategy across the TVET STEPS:

MAYA© ChatGPT

TVET STEPS	CHINA Description and Explanation	Rating
SkillsFirst	Focuses on hands-on training at vocational schools, often starting immediately after lower secondary education.	Strong
SkillsFusion	Integrates theoretical and practical training, with a strong emphasis on aligning with industry needs, especially in manufacturing and technology sectors.	Strong
SkillsForward	Encourages innovation through industry collaborations, particularly in advanced manufacturing and digital technologies, offering graduate-level qualifications and research opportunities.	Very Strong
SkillsAdapt	Actively promotes upskilling and reskilling through lifelong learning initiatives, adapting to changes in the economy and labor market.	Strong

China's approach to TVET is robust, with a comprehensive strategy that effectively addresses each stage from foundational skills to advanced innovation and lifelong learning. The strong alignment with industry needs and the emphasis on continual learning are particularly noteworthy, ensuring that the workforce remains adaptable and competitive.

CASE #5: MALAYSIA

Malaysia's TVET strategy across the TVET STEPS:

TVET STEPS	Description of Malaysia's Strategy	Rating
SkillsFirst	Malaysia has made significant investments in hands-on vocational training centers that are well aligned with industry needs.	Strong
SkillsFusion	The curriculum in Malaysian vocational training integrates both theoretical and practical elements effectively, preparing students well for the workforce.	Strong
SkillsForward	While Malaysia has initiatives aimed at fostering innovation, including some industry PhD programs, these are less developed compared to global leaders like Germany.	Medium
SkillsAdapt	Malaysia is promoting upskilling and reskilling through various programs, but these initiatives could be more widespread and accessible.	Medium

Explanation:

- **SkillsFirst**: Malaysia excels in providing comprehensive hands-on training that aligns well with industry requirements, which is indicative of a strong implementation under the TVETSTEPS R criteria.
- **SkillsFusion**: The integration of theoretical knowledge with practical training is effective, ensuring good industry

relevance and preparing students for real-world applications, meeting the criteria for a strong rating.

- **SkillsForward**: Malaysia's focus on innovation is present but still developing. The existence of some industry PhD programs and collaborations indicates progress, but it's not as extensive or mature as in countries with very strong innovation ecosystems, thus earning a medium rating.
- **SkillsAdapt**: Efforts in lifelong learning are in place, but the reach and effectiveness of these programs are not as comprehensive as they could be, warranting a medium rating.

3.11 TVET STEPS and The African Nations

Evaluating TVET strategies across African nations also requires acknowledging the diverse levels of development, resources, and focus on vocational education within the continent. Here, I'll provide a general assessment using the TVETSTEPS R rubric, focusing on typical features across a broad range of African countries:

MAYA@ ChatGPT

TVET STEPS	General Description of African Nations' Strategy	Rating
SkillsFirst	Many African countries are investing in vocational training, though quality and industry alignment vary significantly across the continent.	Medium
SkillsFusion	Efforts to integrate theoretical and practical training exist but are often hindered by resource constraints and infrastructure limitations.	Medium
SkillsForward	There are pockets of innovation, particularly in countries with better-resourced educational systems, but widespread implementation is limited.	Medium
SkillsAdapt	Initiatives for lifelong learning and skills development are emerging, but consistent and effective implementation remains a challenge.	Medium

Explanation:

- **SkillsFirst**: While there is a commitment to developing vocational training, the execution and quality vary, with some nations having well-developed programs and others still in early stages.
- **SkillsFusion**: Integration of theory and practice is recognized as important, but challenges such as funding, teacher training, and educational materials often impact the effectiveness of these programs.
- **SkillsForward**: Innovation in TVET is growing, especially in more economically stable countries. However, for many nations, these innovations are not yet at the stage where they significantly impact the broader educational landscape.
- **SkillsAdapt**: Although there is an increasing awareness of the importance of lifelong learning, the infrastructure and systems to support it comprehensively are not yet widespread.

To have a better look at how some nations fare within these region, let view several cases form this region.

CASE #1: KENYA

Kenya TVET strategy across the TVET STEPS:

MAYA@ ChatGPT

TVET STEPS	Description of Kenya's Strategy	Rating
SkillsFirst	Kenya has established a strong network of vocational training institutions, which are well-aligned with key economic sectors.	Strong
SkillsFusion	The integration of theoretical knowledge with practical training is increasing, though quality can vary by region and institution.	Medium
SkillsForward	Kenya is actively promoting innovation through partnerships with industries, particularly in technology and agriculture sectors.	Strong
SkillsAdapt	There are several initiatives aimed at lifelong learning and skills development, supported by the government, yet coverage can be uneven.	Medium

Explanation:

- **SkillsFirst**: Kenya's emphasis on practical, hands-on training that meets the needs of its growing economy, particularly in agriculture and technology, merits a strong rating.
- **SkillsFusion**: Efforts to blend theoretical and practical learning are underway, with some institutions leading the

way. However, more consistency across the board is needed.

- **SkillsForward**: Kenya shows strong innovation in its TVET programs, especially through initiatives that link training with emerging industries and technologies.
- **SkillsAdapt**: While there are policies in place for continuous learning and adaptation to new skills, the effectiveness and reach of these programs vary, leading to a medium rating.

CASE #2: SOUTH AFRICA

South Africa's TVET strategy across the TVET STEPS:

MAYA ChatGPT

TVET STEPS	Description of South Africa's Strategy	Rating
SkillsFirst	South Africa has a well-established network of TVET colleges that provide practical, hands-on training aligned with industry needs.	Strong
SkillsFusion	The integration of theoretical and practical training is a focus, but the effectiveness varies significantly across institutions.	Medium
SkillsForward	South Africa shows a commitment to innovation, particularly through collaborations with industry sectors like manufacturing and mining.	Medium
SkillsAdapt	Initiatives for lifelong learning and upskilling are part of the national education policy, but implementation can be uneven.	Medium

Explanation:

- **SkillsFirst**: South Africa excels in providing robust practical training through its extensive network of TVET colleges, strongly aligned with the needs of its diverse economic sectors.
- **SkillsFusion**: There are ongoing efforts to blend theoretical knowledge with practical applications effectively. However, the quality and delivery of this integration can be inconsistent, which impacts the overall success of these programs.
- **SkillsForward**: The country is proactive in promoting innovation within its TVET system, especially in collaboration with key industries. However, these initiatives are not yet widespread or impactful enough to earn a higher rating.
- **SkillsAdapt**: South Africa recognizes the importance of lifelong learning and has policies aimed at promoting it. Still, the reach and effectiveness of these programs are variable, leading to a medium rating.

3.12 TVET STEPS and The Oceania Nations

In evaluating the TVET strategies of nations in Oceania, it's important to note that this region includes a diverse group of countries, from highly developed nations like Australia and New Zealand to smaller island nations with varying levels of resources and development. Here, I'll focus on the general trends in TVET across more developed nations in the region, such as Australia, given their comprehensive and structured TVET systems:

MAYA© ChatGPT

TVET STEPS	Description of Oceania's Strategy (Focusing on Australia and New Zealand)	Rating
SkillsFirst	Both countries offer comprehensive vocational training programs through TAFEs and polytechnics, well-aligned with industry needs, especially in sectors like healthcare and IT.	Very Strong
SkillsFusion	There is a strong emphasis on integrating theoretical knowledge with practical training, supported by a robust national training framework in both countries.	Very Strong
SkillsForward	Both nations are proactive in fostering innovation through R&D, industry partnerships, and support for emerging industries, though New Zealand could enhance this further.	Strong
SkillsAdapt	Lifelong learning is encouraged through various continuing education programs and upskilling initiatives, although access can vary, especially in more remote areas.	Strong

Explanation:

- **SkillsFirst**: Australia and New Zealand excel in providing practical, hands-on training that is highly relevant to the needs of their workforces. This training is supported by well-funded and well-managed institutions.
- **SkillsFusion**: The educational systems in both countries successfully blend theoretical learning with practical applications, ensuring that students are well-prepared for employment.
- **SkillsForward**: Innovation is a key focus, particularly in Australia, which invests heavily in technology and new methodologies in vocational training. New Zealand also supports innovation but has potential for more growth in this area.
- **SkillsAdapt**: Both countries place a significant emphasis on lifelong learning, with extensive programs aimed at upskilling and reskilling. However, the reach of these programs can sometimes be limited in rural and remote areas.

To have a better look at how some nations fare within these region, let view several cases form this region.

CASE #1: AUSTRALIA

Australia's TVET strategy across the TVET STEPS:

MAYA@ ChatGPT

TVET STEPS	Description of Australia's Strategy	Rating
SkillsFirst	Australia's vocational training is highly comprehensive, well-funded, and aligned with industry demands, particularly in trades and services.	Very Strong
SkillsFusion	The integration of theoretical education with practical training is exemplary, facilitated by a robust framework and quality standards.	Very Strong
SkillsForward	Australia is proactive in incorporating innovation and technology in vocational training, maintaining strong ties with industry leaders.	Very Strong
SkillsAdapt	Lifelong learning and professional development are strongly supported through various programs, though access can vary regionally.	Strong

Explanation:

- **SkillsFirst**: Australia excels in providing practical, hands-on training that is highly relevant to the needs of its workforce. This is supported by Technical and Further Education (TAFE) institutions and numerous private RTOs (Registered Training Organizations) across the country.
- **SkillsFusion**: The country's educational institutions seamlessly blend theoretical knowledge with practical skills, ensuring that students are well-prepared for their careers. This is underpinned by a national qualifications framework that enforces high standards.
- **SkillsForward**: Innovation is a key aspect of the Australian TVET system, with ongoing efforts to integrate the latest technologies and teaching methodologies into the curriculum, thereby keeping pace with global trends and industry demands.
- **SkillsAdapt**: Australia places a significant emphasis on lifelong learning, with extensive programs aimed at upskilling and reskilling. While these programs are generally effective, there are opportunities to enhance their reach and consistency across more remote areas.

CASE#2: NEW ZEALAND

New Zealand's TVET strategy across the TVET STEPS:

MAYA@ ChatGPT

TVET STEPS	Description of New Zealand's Strategy	Rating
SkillsFirst	New Zealand has a comprehensive network of Institutes of Technology and Polytechnics (ITPs) providing high-quality, hands-on vocational training.	Strong
SkillsFusion	There is a strong emphasis on integrating theoretical learning with practical training, supported by a well-structured educational framework.	Strong
SkillsForward	New Zealand is proactive in incorporating sustainability and digital technologies into TVET, fostering innovation and responsiveness to industry needs.	Strong
SkillsAdapt	Lifelong learning is supported through various continuing education programs and professional development opportunities, though there is room for wider access.	Strong

Explanation:

- **SkillsFirst**: New Zealand's vocational training is thorough and well-aligned with the needs of both local and international markets, especially in key sectors like agriculture, tourism, and technology.
- **SkillsFusion**: The educational system effectively blends theoretical education with practical skills, ensuring that learners are well-prepared for employment. This is achieved through a curriculum that balances classroom learning with real-world application.

- **SkillsForward**: Innovation is a hallmark of the New Zealand TVET system, with a particular focus on emerging technologies and sustainable practices, which are increasingly important in today's job markets.
- **SkillsAdapt**: New Zealand has a strong focus on lifelong learning, with numerous programs aimed at upskilling and reskilling the workforce. However, there could be improvements in ensuring these opportunities are accessible to all segments of the population, particularly in more remote areas.

Overall, New Zealand's TVET system is robust, with strong performance across all stages of the TVETSTEPS R framework. The system is well-equipped to prepare learners for current and future workforce demands, though it could benefit from expanded access to continuing education and professional development programs.

3.13 TVET STEPS and The Middle East Nations

Evaluating TVET strategies across Middle Eastern nations requires recognizing the diversity within the region, as different countries have varying levels of development, resources, and focus on vocational education. However, I'll provide a general assessment using the TVETSTEPS rubric, focusing on typical features across these nations:

MAYA@ ChatGPT

TVET STEPS	General Description of Middle East Nations' Strategy	Rating
SkillsFirst	Several countries have invested significantly in vocational training, with a particular focus on aligning training with key industries like oil and gas, construction, and hospitality.	Strong
SkillsFusion	There is growing interest in integrating theoretical and practical training, but execution varies widely between countries and institutions.	Medium
SkillsForward	Some nations, particularly those with larger economies, are promoting innovation through education-industry linkages, but this is not uniformly strong across the region.	Medium
SkillsAdapt	There are efforts to promote lifelong learning and skills development, supported by national visions and reforms, yet implementation is inconsistent.	Medium

Explanation:

- **SkillsFirst**: Countries like the UAE, Saudi Arabia, and Qatar have developed robust vocational training programs that are well-aligned with their economic needs, particularly in their dominant sectors. This strategic alignment generally merits a "Strong" rating.
- **SkillsFusion**: There is a push towards blending theoretical knowledge with practical applications, influenced by reforms in higher education and vocational training. However, the effectiveness of these efforts varies significantly across the region, leading to a "Medium" rating.
- **SkillsForward**: Initiatives aimed at fostering innovation are evident, particularly in more economically diversified countries. However, the overall impact and scope of these initiatives are not as comprehensive as seen in global leaders, which leads to a "Medium" rating.
- **SkillsAdapt**: Lifelong learning programs are part of many national strategies (like Saudi Vision 2030 or UAE Vision 2021), aiming to enhance workforce adaptability and

skills. However, the reach and effectiveness of these initiatives are mixed, thus receiving a "Medium" rating.

This evaluation reflects a region that is actively working to improve and expand its TVET capabilities, with some nations further along than others. While there are strong efforts in specific areas, especially in alignment with major industries, more uniformity and development are needed in the integration of educational strategies, innovation support, and lifelong learning programs.

To have a better look at how some nations fare within these region, let view several cases form this region.

CASE #1: QATAR

Qatar's TVET strategy across the TVET STEPS:

MAYA@ ChatGPT

TVET STEPS	Description of Qatar's Strategy	Rating
SkillsFirst	Qatar has established a range of vocational training centres that provide quality training, particularly in industries like construction, IT, and services.	Strong
SkillsFusion	There is a concerted effort to integrate theoretical learning with practical applications, supported by state-of-the-art facilities.	Strong
SkillsForward	Qatar emphasizes innovation in TVET, with investments in technology and partnerships with international educational institutions.	Strong
SkillsAdapt	Initiatives for lifelong learning and career advancement are present, but there's room to expand their reach and inclusivity.	Medium

Explanation:

- **SkillsFirst**: Qatar's vocational training facilities are well-equipped and offer specialized programs tailored to key economic sectors. The quality of hands-on training is generally high, reflecting strong alignment with industry needs.
- **SkillsFusion**: Efforts to blend theoretical and practical learning are effective, facilitated by collaborations with

international partners that bring diverse expertise and pedagogical approaches to the training programs.

- **SkillsForward**: The country is proactive in incorporating new technologies and innovative practices into its TVET programs, aiming to keep pace with global advancements and local economic developments.
- **SkillsAdapt**: While there are several programs aimed at promoting lifelong learning and skill development, these could be more comprehensive and accessible to ensure they meet the needs of all segments of the population.

CASE #2: SAUDI ARABIA

Saudi Arabia's TVET strategy across the TVET STEPS:

MAYA@ ChatGPT

TVET STEPS	Description of Saudi Arabia's Strategy	Rating
SkillsFirst	Saudi Arabia has invested heavily in developing state-of-the-art vocational training centres, especially in sectors like petrochemicals and technology.	Strong
SkillsFusion	The integration of theoretical and practical training is supported by collaborations with global institutions, though consistency varies.	Medium
SkillsForward	There is a strong emphasis on innovation and technology, including investments in new training programs and facilities.	Strong
SkillsAdapt	Saudi Arabia is promoting lifelong learning through initiatives like the Saudi Vision 2030, but the reach and impact are still expanding.	Medium

Explanation:

- **SkillsFirst**: Saudi Arabia's investment in vocational training infrastructure is significant, creating high-quality programs tailored to meet the demands of its economy, particularly in strategic sectors.
- **SkillsFusion**: Efforts to merge theoretical knowledge with practical application are evident, supported by international partnerships that enhance the curriculum. However, the level of integration and effectiveness can vary across different programs and regions.
- **SkillsForward**: The focus on incorporating innovation into TVET is evident, with substantial funding directed towards modernizing training methods and facilities, especially in emerging technologies.
- **SkillsAdapt**: Saudi Arabia recognizes the importance of continuous learning and skills development as part of its broader economic transformation goals. Initiatives are in place, but they are in the process of reaching their full potential and effectiveness.

3.14 TVET STEPS across the World

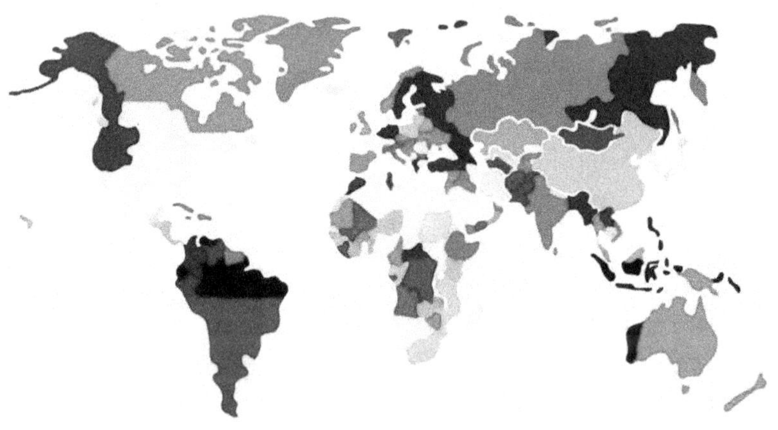

Country	TVET STEPS STATUS	Remarks
Germany	**High	Comprehensive system
Switzerland	High	Dual system leadership
Finland	Medium High	Strong educational focus
UK	Medium High	Varied regional systems
Japan	High	Integrated with technology
South Korea	High	Robust and competitive
Singapore	High	Advanced and specialized
Indonesia	Medium Low	Developing, more focus needed
Malaysia	Medium High	Progressive, developing structure
China	Medium High	Large scale, uneven quality
Kenya	Entry Status	Early stages of development
South Africa	Medium Low	Diverse, implementation varies
UAE	Medium High	Heavy investment in infrastructure
Qatar	Medium High	Focused on skill diversification
Australia	Medium High	Strong but isolated
New Zealand	Medium High	Well-integrated into education
Thailand	Medium Low	Evolving, policy driven
Sri Lanka	Medium Low	Focused on growth, lacks resources
Myanmar	Entry Status	Nascent system, in early stages
Zimbabwe	Entry Status	Limited by economic challenges
USA	Medium High	Highly decentralized

****High:** Having mostly a Strong/Very Strong indication across all four continuum point in the TVET STEPS Rubric.

IMPORTANT: The table presents an informed overview, grounded in typical characteristics observed in each country's TVET systems, reflecting their developmental stage, industry integration, and innovation in vocational training. While some assumptions in the analysis may be generalized, the results are based on credible insights into the respective TVET landscapes. For a more detailed and precise evaluation, additional specific data and insights regarding the current performance of each country's TVET system would enhance the accuracy and depth of the analysis.

3.15 Chapter 3: Your Take-Away

Your Take-Away is Ready!

The TVET STEPS Framework presents a comprehensive, structured approach to understanding and enhancing Technical and Vocational Education and Training (TVET). Designed as a continuum, it highlights the progression of learning from foundational skills to advanced specialization and lifelong career adaptability.

The four key phases—SkillsFirst, SkillsFusion, SkillsForward, and SkillsAdapt—address different stages of career development, ensuring that individuals acquire both practical skills and theoretical knowledge while fostering innovation and adaptability.

The TVET STEPS framework not only guides the design and implementation of effective programs but also assists in refining the definition of TVET. Traditionally viewed as a purely hands-on learning model, TVET is often misunderstood or narrowly defined. By categorizing TVET as a continuum, the framework expands this definition to encompass both practical skills and intellectual engagement. It illustrates how TVET includes theoretical knowledge, critical thinking, research, and the capacity to adapt throughout one's career. This broader understanding can help policymakers and planners communicate TVET's full scope, aligning it with future workforce needs and eliminating misconceptions that might limit strategic planning.

For policymakers, the TVET STEPS model offers a strategic tool for designing programs that align with labor market demands and industry standards. Each phase in the framework allows for targeted interventions to enhance workforce readiness, ensuring students are prepared for both current jobs and emerging career fields. Incorporating continuous learning opportunities through SkillsAdapt ensures that workers can stay competitive in rapidly changing industries.

For planners and strategists, the framework emphasizes the importance of resource allocation and infrastructure development. Implementing TVET STEPS requires investments in educator training, modern facilities, and curriculum development that balance theory and practice. A flexible, adaptable TVET system can help nations meet specific economic and cultural needs, avoiding a one-size-fits-all approach.

By expanding the definition of TVET and illustrating its multifaceted nature, the TVET STEPS model empowers stakeholders to build resilient, future-ready workforces that contribute to sustainable economic growth and innovation.

Lastly, here are 5 major conclusions:

- TVET is a continuous learning pathway, not just hands-on training.
- The TVET STEPS Framework offers a structured approach to career progression.
- SkillsForward drives innovation, leadership, and technological advancements in TVET.
- SkillsAdapt ensures professionals stay relevant with lifelong learning.
- Successful implementation of TVET STEPS requires investment in training and infrastructure.

The TVET VARIANTS

Chapter 4: The TVET Variants

What's in a name?

Quite a lot, as it turns out, especially when it comes to the diverse and dynamic field of vocational and technical education. Across different countries and regions, this educational sector adopts various names—each reflecting specific local needs, economic goals, and cultural contexts.

This chapter looks at TVET from a nomenclature perspective: The Names/Variants of TVET. This variety in nomenclature isn't just about regional preferences; it represents tailored approaches to preparing individuals for the workforce.

In the rich tapestry of vocational and technical education, the names we assign to different programs and systems are like the vibrant hues of a butterfly's wings.

Each name, carefully chosen to encapsulate the essence of its educational approach, reflects the unique characteristics and aspirations of its respective region or community. Just as the diversity of butterflies enriches our natural world, the varieties of TVET names enrich our educational landscape, offering tailored pathways to success in the global workforce.

As we explore this landscape, we delve into why these varied names exist and what they signify about the educational models they describe. In our next discussion, we will be introduced to these names and the distinct educational products they represent, unravelling the intricate stories behind them and discovering their significance in shaping the future of vocational and technical education worldwide.

Three Questions

Based on the readings of this chapter. These are important questions to prompt critical thinking among policymakers, politicians, and TVET strategists as they plan their local TVET initiatives:

1. **Adaptation to Local Needs:** How can you ensure that the chosen TVET variant aligns with the specific economic and cultural needs of your region? What local factors (such as industry presence, labour market demands, and cultural values) will influence your choice of TVET model?
2. **International Collaboration and Benchmarking:** Considering the global landscape of TVET, what strategies will you implement to learn from international best practices while avoiding the pitfalls of merely replicating models that may not fit your local context?
3. **Measuring Success:** What metrics and evaluation processes will you establish to assess the effectiveness of the TVET programs? How will you measure the impact of TVET on both individual career success and broader economic development?

4.1 The Variations of TVET

In the natural world, the variation of butterflies—from their vibrant colours to their patterns and sizes—illustrates the beauty and necessity of diversity within a species, allowing for adaptation to various environments and survival strategies. Similarly, in the realm of education, particularly in Technical and Vocational Education and Training (TVET), a spectrum of variations exists, each tailored to meet specific regional and industrial needs effectively.

Just as no single type of butterfly dominates the entire spectrum of habitats, no one model of TVET can suit all educational and workforce requirements globally. These variations, including VET (Vocational Education and Training), CTE (Career and Technical Education), TET (Technical Education and Training), TVSD (Technical and Vocational Skills Development), PTET (Professional and Technical Education and Training), and FET (Further Education and Training), cater to diverse learning styles, economic contexts, and industry demands.

Each TVET model has a unique focus as we shall see. The existence of these variations is crucial. They allow educational systems to adapt to the evolving demands of the global economy, much like butterflies adapt to their surroundings. Each TVET model's unique features ensure that education remains relevant and aligned with both current and future needs, promoting sustained economic growth and individual career success.

4.2 TVET Variant One: VET

> *"It offers immediate job readiness through hands-on training in a range of trades and industries."*

Vocational Education and Training (VET). VET focuses on providing entry-level vocational education to young individuals (typically aged 15 years and older). It offers immediate job readiness through hands-on training in a range of trades and industries. The programs vary in duration and occur from secondary to post-secondary levels, aiming to equip fresh students with the necessary skills for initial employment in their chosen fields.

Venue: Often takes place in dedicated vocational schools, technical institutes, or through apprenticeship programs in secondary or post-secondary institutions. Some VET programs may also be offered at community colleges or specialized vocational training centers.

Historically, VET can be traced as follows:

- **Who & When**: Developed by various national education systems over many decades.
- **Why**: VET was established to provide direct job skills training for specific trades and professions,

addressing the immediate needs of industrializing economies.

- **How**: Names and frameworks were formalized as countries industrialized and recognized the need for a skilled workforce tailored to rapidly developing sectors.

VET, real world example/s:

<u>Scenario: Culinary Arts Program in Australia</u>

1. **Program Setup**: A VET culinary arts program is established in partnership with local restaurants and hotels to provide hands-on training.
2. **Skills Development**: Students learn food preparation, kitchen management, and customer service under the guidance of experienced chefs.
3. **Internship Placement**: Students complete internships at prestigious restaurants, gaining real-world experience.
4. **Employment Outcome**: Graduates are often hired directly from their internship placements, reflecting the program's effectiveness in meeting industry needs.

4.3 TVET Variant Two: TET

"TET ... is more narrowly focused on technical and engineering disciplines (STEM) ... "

Technical Education and Training (TET). TET is similar to CTE but specifically focuses on more technical fields, offering training from entry to advanced levels. The programs are tailored for fresh student's post-secondary education, providing immediate skills applicable in technical and industrial sectors. TET is designed to prepare students for direct entry into technical professions. It is more narrowly focused on technical and engineering disciplines (STEM), catering primarily to those entering technical fields where specific skills are required.

Venue: Usually occurs in technical and polytechnic institutes, and at universities that offer specialized programs in engineering and technology. These are predominantly post-secondary settings.

Historically, TET can be traced as follows:

- **Who & When**: Developed by educational institutions worldwide, particularly in regions focusing on engineering and technology.
- **Why**: To cater to the needs of emerging industries and technological sectors requiring specialized technical skills.
- **How**: The naming reflects the emphasis on technical skills applicable to industries driven by technology and innovation.

TET, real world example/s:

Scenario: Engineering Program in Germany

1. **Program Setup**: A TET program offers advanced mechanical engineering training, closely aligned with automotive manufacturing needs.
2. **Collaboration with Industry**: Automotive companies sponsor projects and provide equipment, ensuring training remains cutting-edge.
3. **Skill Application**: Students participate in designing and producing parts for new vehicle models, showcasing their high-level technical skills.
4. **Career Progression**: Graduates enter the workforce with high competence, driving innovation and efficiency in automotive manufacturing.

4.4 TVET Variant Three: TVSD

"TVSD focuses on the continuous development of vocational skills... offers training that is immediately applicable within the workplace..."

Technical and Vocational Skills Development (TVSD). Primarily for adult employees already in the workforce, TVSD focuses on the continuous development of vocational skills. It offers training that is immediately applicable within the workplace, helping employees upgrade and refine their skills to meet evolving job requirements. The training occurs within the working environment and varies in duration based on specific skill demands.

Venue: Conducted within the workplace or in training centers closely linked to specific industries. TVSD is often part of on-the-job training programs or continuous professional development courses offered by employers.

Historically, TVSD can be traced as follows:

- **Who & When**: Often shaped by international agencies like UNESCO and individual national education policies.
- **Why**: To highlight the ongoing development of skills that are necessary for economic adaptation and workforce flexibility.
- **How**: The name emphasizes skill development as a continuous process rather than a one-time educational phase.

TVSD, real world example/s:

Scenario: Renewable Energy Skills Program in India

1. **Program Setup**: A TVSD program focuses on solar panel installation and maintenance.
2. **Skills Training**: Participants receive training on the latest solar technologies, safety protocols, and troubleshooting.
3. **Government Incentives**: The program is supported by government subsidies to promote renewable energy jobs.
4. **Impact on Community**: Many graduates set up their businesses or work for local governments, leading to widespread adoption of solar energy in their communities.

4.5 TVET Variant Four: FET

> *"FET focuses on delayed job readiness, allowing learners to deepen or diversify their skills at a post-secondary level."*

Further Education and Training (FET). Targeted at adult employees, FET is designed to provide advanced training or career transition opportunities. These programs are typically pursued post-employment or alongside working, helping adults to enhance or shift their career paths. FET focuses on delayed job readiness, allowing learners to deepen or diversify their skills at a post-secondary level. It is broader and more diverse, providing educational opportunities across a variety of fields and is geared towards adults seeking career advancement or a shift in their professional path.

Venue: Generally offered at community colleges, technical institutes, adult education centers, and sometimes universities. These programs are specifically tailored for adults, often taking place in evening classes or part-time formats to accommodate working individuals.

Historically, FET can be traced as follows:

- **Who & When**: This model has been particularly prominent in countries like the UK and South Africa, where it serves as a bridge between secondary education and higher education or employment.
- **Why**: To facilitate a smooth transition to higher education and to cater to non-university-bound students with vocational training.
- **How**: The name "further education" indicates that it extends beyond traditional schooling without necessarily leading to university education.

FET, real world example/s:

Scenario: Healthcare Transition Program in South Africa

1. **Program Setup**: An FET program focuses on healthcare, preparing students for both employment and further medical studies.
2. **Bridge to Higher Education**: Courses are designed to meet prerequisites for medical school, alongside training in practical nursing skills.
3. **Community Health Impact**: Many graduates work in local clinics while pursuing further education, improving community health outcomes.
4. **Long-Term Career Development**: The program supports a continuous pipeline of healthcare professionals critical to regional health services.

4.6 TVET Variant Five: CTE

"CTE offers comprehensive technical education from entry to advanced levels for fresh students."

Career and Technical Education (CTE). CTE offers comprehensive technical education from entry to advanced levels for fresh students. It prepares students for a range of technical careers through a combination of foundational skills and potential progression to more complex competencies. CTE programs are designed to provide both immediate and future job opportunities, and they take place from secondary to post-secondary education settings.

Venue: Typically conducted in high schools (secondary education) and post-secondary institutions like technical colleges. CTE programs are sometimes integrated within comprehensive high schools or specialized CTE centers.

Historically, CTE can be traced as follows:

- **Who & When**: In the United States, what is now called CTE began to take shape with the Smith-Hughes Act of 1917.
- **Why**: The aim was to formalize and fund vocational education at the high school level to prepare students for entry into the workforce.
- **How**: Over time, the term "vocational education" was largely replaced by "career and technical education" to reflect a broader educational scope and a focus on career readiness that includes college preparation.

CTE, real world example/s:

Scenario: Technology Integration in U.S. High Schools

1. **Program Setup**: A high school in the USA integrates CTE focused on information technology, offering courses in coding, network administration, and cybersecurity.
2. **Industry Certification**: Courses are aligned with industry certifications; which students can earn alongside their high school diplomas.
3. **Post-Graduation Paths**: Graduates proceed to tech jobs, higher education in STEM fields, or start their tech enterprises.
4. **Long-Term Impact**: The program boosts local tech industry growth and student career success.

4.7 TVET Variant Six: PTET

"PTET is more aligned with professional development and advanced technical training,"

PTET stands for Professional Technical Education and Training. It is a framework or approach that focuses on providing advanced technical and professional education. Unlike traditional TVET, which often centres around entry-level or intermediate skills for specific trades, PTET is more aligned with professional development and advanced technical training, often catering to sectors that require higher-level qualifications.

PTET is typically designed for industries or sectors that demand a combination of technical expertise and professional-level competencies. It involves more specialized training that may lead to higher-level qualifications like bachelor's degrees, master's degrees, or professional certifications. This approach is especially relevant in fields such as engineering, information technology, biotechnology, and healthcare, where a higher level of expertise is required.

While TVET focuses on vocational skills, PTET emphasizes professional-level education and lifelong learning, often aligning more with the needs of advanced industries and innovation-driven economies.

Venue: Primarily takes place in professional training institutes, through corporate training programs, and at workplaces. It is also common in specialized institutes that offer certification and advanced professional qualifications.

Historically, PTET can be traced as follows:

- **Who & When**: Professional Technical Education and Training (PTET) was developed by the World Federation of Colleges and Polytechnics (WFCP) as a strategic framework to address the evolving demands of modern economies and the need for a more skilled and adaptable workforce.
- **Why:** Formalizing Advanced TVET - The term PTET was introduced to bring global recognition to this more advanced, professional side of vocational education, allowing different countries to categorize and develop high-level technical education under a unified framework.
- **How**: PTET reflects the dual focus on professional and technical education within a single framework.

PTET, real world example/s:

Scenario: Financial Services Academy in the UK

1. **Program Setup**: A PTET program collaborates with financial firms to offer training in financial analysis, management, and regulatory compliance.
2. **Professional Qualifications**: The program includes pathways to earn chartered financial analyst certifications.
3. **Career Readiness**: Graduates enter the finance sector with advanced skills, significantly reducing on-the-job training time.
4. **Sector Influence**: Alumni frequently advance to senior roles, influencing industry practices and standards.

The World Federation of Colleges and Polytechnics (WFPC)

The World Federation of Colleges and Polytechnics (WFCP) is an international network comprising colleges, institutes, polytechnics, and associations of vocational education providers from around the globe. The WFCP serves as a platform for these institutions to collaborate, exchange knowledge, and share best practices in vocational and technical education. Its mission is to advocate for the critical role that vocational training plays in the global economy, aiming to enhance the skills and training standards across nations. By facilitating connections and fostering educational partnerships, the WFCP contributes to workforce development, helping to address skill shortages and enhance employability for students worldwide.

The relationship between PTET and The World Federation of Colleges and Polytechnics (WFCP) is significant because WFCP serves as a global network that advocates for professional and technical education systems worldwide. It connects educational institutions and stakeholders across the globe, promoting best practices, enhancing skill development, and supporting the goals of PTET through international collaboration. WFCP's commitment to advancing TVET aligns closely with the aims of PTET by facilitating knowledge exchange, fostering international partnerships, and enhancing the global capabilities of the workforce.

4.8 An Umbrella called TVET

So how does TVET fit into all of this?

TVET serves as a broad umbrella term that encompasses six(6) the specialized training formats; VET, FET, TET, CTE, TVSD, and PTET. Each of these acronyms represents a distinct approach or focus within the wider field of vocational education, catering to diverse needs and contexts.

However, the term TVET itself, while useful for general categorization, often proves too generic to capture the nuanced differences and specific orientations of its subsets. This generic nature can pose challenges for policymakers, educators, and strategists who are tasked with developing and refining training programs.

These nuanced differences are crucial in shaping TVET strategies that are accurately tailored to meet the evolving demands of the workforce and industries.

Thus, for policymakers, educators, and strategists in the field, understanding the specific attributes and target outcomes of each variant is crucial. This nuanced understanding helps in designing more effective programs and policies that are better suited to meet specific local or sectoral needs, rather than applying a one-size-fits-all approach that a broad use of the term TVET might imply.

Understanding the distinctions among TVET's various forms is essential for effective policy formulation and program implementation. It ensures that training programs are not only relevant but also aligned with specific economic, cultural, and educational needs of a region or sector.

4.9 The TVET Variant Continuum

Understanding the continuum of TVET is essential because it provides a structured framework for identifying the educational needs and opportunities at different stages of an individual's career and life.

This understanding helps in designing targeted training programs that are not only sequential but also adaptive to the evolving demands of the workforce and industries.

The continuum can be understood as such, TVET as an umbrella term, where VET begins as the first point of the continuum, followed through by the other variants as indicated below. PTET is the final point as it is seen as preparing for an advance and innovative version of TVET.

In a nutshell, a continuum of TVET Variants can be seen below:

What if we were to match it with TVET STEPS?

Here a table comparing the <u>TVET STEPS</u> to their closest <u>TVET Variants</u> based on educational progression and the skills they focus on:

TVET STEP	TVET Variant	Description
SkillsFirst	**VET**	Focuses on acquiring **basic vocational skills** and hands-on training, preparing learners for entry-level roles in industries. Similar to VET, this step emphasizes quick job readiness through practical skills.
SkillsFusion	**CTE, FET**	Blends **theoretical knowledge** with **practical skills**, offering a balanced approach. CTE and FET focus on career and technical education with a mix of practical and theoretical components, aimed at broader career growth.
SkillsForward	**TET, PTET**	Emphasizes **advanced specialization**, research, and development. TET and PTET focus on advanced technical skills and research, preparing learners for leadership or specialized roles in industries like engineering, IT, and healthcare.
SkillsAdapt	**TVSD, PTET**	Focuses on **lifelong learning** and adaptability, ensuring that professionals continuously update their skills. TVSD supports ongoing upskilling,

		while PTET allows advanced professionals to stay competitive in evolving industries.

Explanation:

- SkillsFirst matches VET as both focus on entry-level vocational skills.
- SkillsFusion aligns with CTE and FET, blending practical and theoretical knowledge for career growth.
- SkillsForward corresponds to TET and PTET, focusing on advanced technical education and research.
- SkillsAdapt is closely related to TVSD and PTET, as they emphasize continuous learning and upskilling for professionals.

This comparison shows how the **TVET STEPS** align with established TVET variants, mapping the progression from basic skills to advanced, lifelong learning.

4.10 TVET Variants in Flight

"While some nations prefer specialized variants to address particular sectors or skills gaps, others opt for a broader, more encompassing approach labelled simply as TVET."

The landscape of TVET is diverse.

Each different nations adopting various variants such as TET, VET, PTET, FET, CTE, and TVSD to meet specific economic and workforce needs. This diversity in educational frameworks allows each country to tailor its programs to the unique demands of its industries and labour markets, maximizing the effectiveness of its workforce training. While some nations prefer specialized variants to address particular sectors or skills gaps, others opt for a broader, more encompassing approach labelled simply as TVET.

This generic labelling enables a more flexible integration of multiple educational needs and industry requirements under one comprehensive system, supporting a wide range of economic activities and technological advancements. This strategic choice in nomenclature and educational focus reflects the varying priorities and capabilities of nations in harnessing vocational and technical education for economic development and competitiveness.

TVET360 has prepared a table that matches TVET and its variant types with three major countries, both from the East and the West, along with explanations on why these models are adopted in these countries compared to others.

NOTE: Although some countries do have more than one variant being deployed, there is always a dominant type:

Variant	Countries	Reason for Adoption	Focus
TVET	Germany, Singapore, South Korea, Malaysia	Germany's dual system integrates technical and vocational training, focusing on manufacturing, engineering, and other technical fields. Singapore adapts TVET to support its service-oriented and high-tech economy. South Korea focuses on high-tech industries.	Broad focus on both technical and vocational education
VET	Switzerland, Australia, UK	Switzerland's VET is apprenticeship-driven, aimed at practical job-specific skills. Australia's VET supports sectors like hospitality and trades, while the UK focuses on healthcare and construction.	Primarily vocational, with strong industry links
TET	Finland, Japan, USA	Finland and Japan focus on boosting technological innovation. The USA integrates TET with STEM education to enhance technological competitiveness.	Strong focus on technical and technological education
PTET	Netherlands, Canada, USA	Netherlands and Canada focus on professional sectors like environmental science and engineering. In the USA, PTET supports professional qualifications in sectors like healthcare and engineering.	Professional and technical education for specific industries
FET	Ireland, South Africa, New Zealand	FET bridges education gaps and prepares students for employment or further education. New Zealand's FET supports diverse sectors like tourism and agriculture.	Focus on bridging gaps to employment or further education
CTE	USA, Canada, Australia	The USA uses CTE to align education with market needs, focusing on trades and technical careers. Canada and Australia implement CTE for diverse sectors like natural resources and healthcare.	Career-specific technical and vocational training
TVSD	China, India, Vietnam	China and India use TVSD to rapidly train skilled workers for growing industries, while Vietnam focuses on improving manufacturing competitiveness.	Skills development for rapid workforce preparation

This table shows how different countries select and implement TVET models based on their specific economic structures, industry demands, and educational goals. Each model serves distinct purposes, addressing the unique challenges and opportunities within each national context.

Conclusion:

In this updated format, the table better differentiates between variants of TVET, VET, and other systems, clearly distinguishing how Germany focuses on a broader technical and vocational education while Switzerland emphasizes vocational training through its apprenticeship model. Each variant's scope and focus are now clearer, providing a better understanding of how these systems are tailored to local industry needs.

Recall:

- **TVET**: Chosen for its broad applicability, crucial for countries with diverse industrial bases or those focusing on innovation and technology.
- **TET**: Adopted mainly in countries that emphasize technological advancement and high-tech industries.
- **VET**: Popular in countries with a strong tradition of vocational education and significant needs in specific trades.
- **PTET**: Utilized in countries aiming to combine professional training with technical education, often in specialized industries requiring higher education levels.
- **FET**: Used primarily in countries looking to smooth the transition from secondary education to the workforce or further studies, helping to mitigate educational and employment gaps.
- **CTE**: Implemented in countries where there is a need to directly align educational outcomes with specific career paths, enhancing workforce readiness in diverse sectors.

- **TVSD**: Critical in rapidly developing economies that need to quickly scale up their workforce's skills, especially in manufacturing and industrial sectors.

4.11 Variants of the West: Germany

"...the system's (DUAL TVET) rigidity and dependence on economic fluctuations present challenges in terms of flexibility and accessibility."

As an example, Germany's approach to TVET (Technical and Vocational Education and Training) is highly structured and deeply integrated with its industrial sectors, especially within its renowned dual system of vocational training. This system combines classroom-based education at vocational schools with on-the-job training at participating companies. Here is an outline of the key TVET variants in Germany and how they are implemented:

TVET Variant	Key Players	Focus Areas	Purpose
VET (Vocational Education and Training)	Vocational Schools, Companies (Dual System Partners)	Apprenticeships in industrial, commercial, and crafts sectors	To combine theoretical education with practical experience, preparing students directly for the workforce.
FET (Further Education and Training)	Technical Schools, Colleges	Specialized technical and continuing education	To provide deeper knowledge and skills following initial vocational training, enhancing career progression.
TET (Technical Education and Training)	Universities of Applied Sciences, Technical Institutes	Advanced technical education in fields like engineering, IT	To foster high-level technical expertise necessary for Germany's technology-driven sectors.
CTE (Career and Technical Education)	Vocational Colleges, Secondary Schools	Integrated academic and vocational curricula	To equip younger students with early career-oriented skills and a pathway to further education or employment.
PTET (Post-Technical and Vocational Education and Training)	Professional Academies, Master Schools	Highly specialized professional training and master craftsman courses	To offer advanced training and qualifications for professionals aiming to achieve expertise in their trades.
TVSD (Technical and Vocational Skills Development)	Corporate Training Centers, Private Institutions	Upskilling and reskilling of existing workforce	To adapt to technological changes and maintain industrial competitiveness.

Conclusion: *Germany's TVET system is effectively tailored to meet the needs of its robust industrial economy*, emphasizing practical skills and seamless integration into the labor market. The dual system, in particular, is a cornerstone of this approach, ensuring that students receive both theoretical education and practical training directly relevant to their future careers. This strategy not only supports Germany's high standards of industrial productivity but also addresses the skilled labor needs consistently and efficiently. Challenges such as maintaining the quality of training and adapting to rapid technological advancements are met with rigorous standards and continuous updates to curricula, illustrating a well-rounded approach to vocational education and training.

Germany's structured approach to TVET provides numerous advantages but also poses certain challenges.

Below is a table outlining the key advantages and disadvantages of Germany's TVET system:

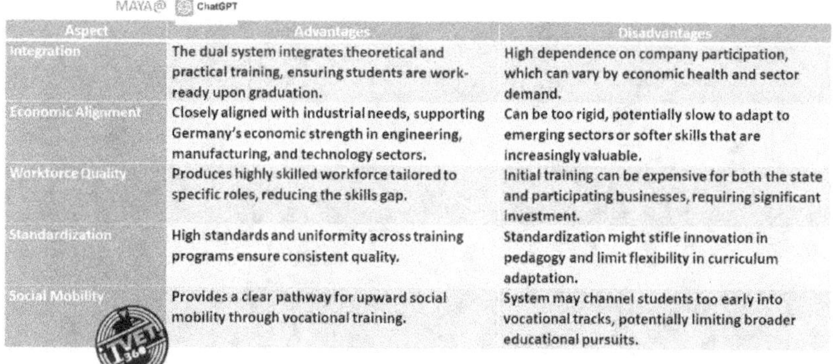
MAYA@ ChatGPT

Aspect	Advantages	Disadvantages
Integration	The dual system integrates theoretical and practical training, ensuring students are work-ready upon graduation.	High dependence on company participation, which can vary by economic health and sector demand.
Economic Alignment	Closely aligned with industrial needs, supporting Germany's economic strength in engineering, manufacturing, and technology sectors.	Can be too rigid, potentially slow to adapt to emerging sectors or softer skills that are increasingly valuable.
Workforce Quality	Produces highly skilled workforce tailored to specific roles, reducing the skills gap.	Initial training can be expensive for both the state and participating businesses, requiring significant investment.
Standardization	High standards and uniformity across training programs ensure consistent quality.	Standardization might stifle innovation in pedagogy and limit flexibility in curriculum adaptation.
Social Mobility	Provides a clear pathway for upward social mobility through vocational training.	System may channel students too early into vocational tracks, potentially limiting broader educational pursuits.

Conclusion: Germany's TVET system is renowned for its efficiency in creating a well-prepared workforce, which is a critical component of the country's economic success, particularly in technical and industrial sectors. The dual system is especially beneficial, providing real-world skills and job readiness. However, the system's rigidity and dependence on economic fluctuations present challenges in terms of flexibility and accessibility. Addressing these issues involves continually adapting the TVET framework to accommodate emerging industries and broader educational goals, ensuring it remains responsive to both economic needs and individual aspirations.

4.12 Variants of the East: Malaysia

"However, the challenges it (Malaysia) faces include managing such a complex system effectively while ensuring that all programs maintain high standards and adapt to future economic changes."

As an example, Malaysia's adaptation to the TVET models involves a diverse array of educational programs that cater to the different needs of its rapidly developing economy.

Different stakeholders in Malaysia focus on various TVET variants to optimize skill development across multiple sectors, such as manufacturing, services, and high-tech industries.

Below is a table that illustrates how various players in Malaysia engage with different TVET models to meet specific educational and economic goals:

TVET Variant	Key Players	Focus Areas	Purpose
VET	Community Colleges, Vocational Schools	Entry-level skills for trades and crafts	To equip students with practical skills for immediate employment in various trades.
FET	Technical Universities, Polytechnics	Bridging courses, undergraduate studies	To provide further education that enhances skills and prepares students for higher technical roles or continued education.
TET	German-Malaysian Institute (GMI), Universities of Technology	Specialized technical education in fields like engineering and technology	To advance technical knowledge and provide high-level skills in specialized sectors such as manufacturing and engineering.
CTE	Secondary Schools, Kolej Vokasional (Specialized Training Centers)	Career-oriented education	To integrate academic and technical learning for seamless transition into the workforce or higher education.
PTET	Technical Universities, Professional Institutes, Advanced Training Facilities	Postgraduate and advanced training	To offer advanced skills and knowledge, facilitating professional growth and specialization.
TVSD	Government Skills Training Institutes	Skills enhancement and upskilling	To quickly adapt to changing industry demands and improve the competitiveness of the workforce.

This table showcases how Malaysia's approach to TVET is both comprehensive and targeted, allowing for a versatile educational landscape that supports continuous learning and adaptation to new technologies and market needs. By diversifying the application of TVET models, Malaysia ensures that it can cater to a broad spectrum of educational and employment requirements, thus supporting the nation's goals for economic development and technological advancement.

Malaysia's diverse approach to implementing various TVET models offers distinct advantages and poses some challenges. Here's a table outlining the key advantages and disadvantages of Malaysia's adaptation to the TVET framework:

Aspect	Advantages	Disadvantages
Comprehensiveness	Covers a wide range of skills and sectors, ensuring that education aligns with various industry needs.	Can lead to complexity in management and coordination across different programs and institutions.
Flexibility	Allows for adaptations based on industry changes and economic demands, facilitating continuous learning.	May result in uneven quality and standards due to the diverse nature of programs and lack of uniformity.
Specialization	Encourages high levels of specialization in areas like technology and advanced manufacturing, driving innovation.	Specialization might neglect broader educational goals, limiting holistic education and general skills.
Economic Alignment	Ensures that training is directly linked to economic sectors in need, boosting employability and relevance.	Overemphasis on current market needs could overlook future shifts and emerging sectors, risking obsolescence.
Resource Utilization	Efficient use of resources by targeting specific sectors and needs, potentially maximizing return on investment.	Diverse focuses can lead to disparities in funding allocation, affecting the quality of training in less prioritized areas.

Malaysia's multifaceted approach to TVET strategically positions it to meet immediate and long-term economic and workforce demands. However, the challenges it faces include managing such a complex system effectively while ensuring that all programs maintain high standards and adapt to future economic changes.

TDC360's Suggestion: Malaysia should strategize its TVET agenda by enhancing coordination among different variants, tailoring programs to regional and sector-specific needs, and investing in quality assurance to maintain standards. A unified policy framework that supports flexibility and adaptability in response to technological advancements and labour market trends is essential.

4.13 The Two Gardens

> *"Both nations are working towards adapting their educational models to better meet the demands of a rapidly changing global economy."*

Comparing Germany and Malaysia's approaches to TVET highlights some similarities in structure but also significant differences in implementation, cultural integration, and industry involvement.

Conclusion: Both Germany and Malaysia recognize the importance of TVET for economic growth and workforce development. Germany's system is distinguished by its high degree of integration with industry, cultural valorisation of vocational training, and comprehensive governmental support.

Malaysia, while having a more varied and less unified system, is making significant strides in enhancing its TVET framework through increased industry collaboration and government initiatives. Malaysia's challenge lies in elevating the perception of TVET to the level seen in Germany and ensuring a cohesive strategy across its diverse programs. Both nations are working towards adapting their educational models to better meet the demands of a rapidly changing global economy.

Below is a table that compares key aspects of the TVET systems in both countries:

Aspect	Germany	Malaysia
Economic Alignment	Highly Synchronized – Deeply integrated with manufacturing and engineering; supports key industries with precisely tailored training; stable and long-term focused.	Evolving Alignment - Increasingly aligns with sectors like technology and services; reactive to market needs, leading to some fragmentation; still developing deeper industry integration.
Industry Collaboration	Extremely strong with mandatory industry partnerships in the dual system.	Growing, with increasing involvement through collaborations and government initiatives.
Cultural Perception	Vocational training is highly respected and considered equivalent to academic pathways.	Gradually gaining respect, though traditionally seen as less prestigious than academic degrees.
Government Support	Extensive with robust financial and regulatory backing.	Significant, with numerous initiatives to enhance skills training and employability.
Flexibility and Adaptation	Systematically adapts to technological and economic changes with high standards.	Adapts to industry needs, but sometimes lacks uniformity and speed in response to changes.
System Structure	Highly structured and comprehensive, covering a wide range of industries.	Diverse and segmented with various programs catering to different industry needs.
Lifelong Learning	Strong focus on continuous learning and professional development.	Increasing focus on lifelong learning, particularly through upskilling and reskilling programs.
Public-Private Partnerships	Deeply ingrained, with businesses actively participating in training and curriculum development.	Expanding, with more businesses engaging in partnerships but not as ingrained as in Germany.

Inclusivity	High due to societal value placed on vocational paths; offers many opportunities for various skill levels.	Working towards greater inclusivity, though challenges remain in reaching rural and underserved communities.

Rest of the World: How do you think they aligning themselves to the variants?

TVET Dominant Variants by Nations

MAYA@ ChatGPT

TVET Variants	Industrial Role	Educational/Institutional Role	Prominent Institutions
VET	Direct skills training for specific industries like manufacturing, construction, and services.	Provide hands-on training and apprenticeships, often in collaboration with industry partners.	TAFE (Australia).
FET	Supports industries requiring a blend of academic and vocational skills, such as tourism and hospitality.	Bridges secondary education to higher education or direct employment, focusing on broader skill sets.	Further Education Colleges (UK), Community Colleges (USA)
TET	Enhances technical capabilities in high-tech industries such as IT, biotechnology, and engineering.	Offers specialized technical training, often at the post-secondary level, with a strong emphasis on STEM.	Institutes of Technology (Ireland), Polytechnics (Singapore)
CTE	Prepares students for careers in sectors needing a mix of technical and soft skills, like healthcare and digital media.	Integrates vocational training with academic curricula at the secondary and post-secondary levels.	Career Academies (USA), Colleges of Further Education (UK)
TVSD	Focuses on upskilling and reskilling employees in rapidly evolving sectors like renewable energy and ICT.	Provides flexible training programs that adapt to changing industry technologies and practices.	Vocational Training Council (Hong Kong), Industrial Training Institutes (India)
PTET	Targets high-level professional industries requiring advanced technical and managerial skills, such as finance and project management.	Combines advanced technical training with professional education, often leading to certifications and degrees.	Fachhochschulen (Austria)

4.14 Chapter 04 - Take-Away

Your Take-Away is ready!

Understanding the variations within the TVET framework is crucial for designing effective, tailored educational programs. By recognizing the distinct roles of TVET models like VET, CTE, TET, TVSD, PTET, and FET, policymakers can align training with specific industry and workforce needs. This alignment not only meets current labour demands but also anticipates future technological shifts.

Efficient resource allocation is a key benefit of this nuanced understanding, allowing for optimized economic and social outcomes. For example, regions focusing on high-tech might prioritize PTET, while those with a hospitality focus could emphasize VET.

For nations with diverse variants in play, they should centralize coordination, standardize quality across TVET variants, tailor programs to regional/sectorial needs, and foster industry collaborations to ensure aligned, effective vocational education systems."

It's interesting to know that VET and FET are particularly popular among many nations because they directly address the practical and immediate needs of the workforce and students:

- **VET** is highly regarded for its direct link to employment and specific skill training, which resonates well in economies with a high demand for skilled labour in specific sectors.
- **FET** offers a crucial educational stepping stone that enhances lifelong learning and provides flexibility for students to navigate their educational and career journeys effectively.

Both VET and FET fill essential roles in the educational landscape, directly contributing to economic development by preparing a skilled workforce and providing individuals with opportunities for personal growth and job satisfaction. These specific benefits make them popular choices among students, educators, and policymakers alike.

In summary, grasping the nuances of TVET models allows strategists and policymakers to develop more responsive, efficient, and inclusive education systems, aligning with both economic needs and broader social goals.

Lastly, here are 5 major conclusions:

- TVET represents a broad range of specialized educational models, each tailored to specific workforce needs.
- Different TVET variants address specific workforce needs and industry demands.
- Effective TVET strategies require aligning programs with local economic and cultural contexts.
- Countries vary in TVET implementation; some lack cohesion and focus.
- Collaboration with industries is essential for maintaining relevance and driving innovation.

The TVET MAESTRO

Chapter 5: The TVET 'MAESTRO"

This chapter looks at TVET from the perspective of a grandmaster of TVET: Germany

Germany, stands as a beacon of economic strength in Europe, celebrated for its precision engineering and robust manufacturing sector. This reputation is underpinned by a commitment to technological innovation and a disciplined approach to business and governance. Central to its success is Germany's mastery over TVET, especially its acclaimed dual system that marries classroom learning with real-world application through apprenticeships. This system is a cornerstone of Germany's educational culture, playing a crucial role in the country's industrial achievements and remarkably low youth unemployment rates.

The sustainability and efficacy of Germany's TVET are upheld by a symphony of collaboration among government, industry, and educational institutions. The government fortifies this system with strategic legislation and funding, while businesses invest in cultivating a future workforce that continues to drive competitive prowess.

Chapter Five (5), titled "The TVET Maestro," will explore this system through the personal academic journeys of its diverse practitioners-to-be —from bakers to graphic designers. These stories will reveal how Germany's expertly conducted TVET system not only shapes individual careers and skillsets but also enhances the nation's economic performance, thus illustrating its profound impact on both personal development and broader societal prosperity.

Three Questions

Based on the readings of this chapter. These are important questions to prompt critical thinking among policymakers, politicians, and TVET strategists as they plan their local TVET initiatives:

1. **Legislative Frameworks:** Considering the foundational role of governmental support in Germany's TVET success, what specific legislative measures and funding models will you establish to sustain and enhance the efficacy of TVET programs in your region?
2. **Cultural and Economic Adaptation:** How can you adapt aspects of Germany's dual system to fit the unique cultural, economic, and industrial contexts of your country? What modifications might be necessary to accommodate different levels of industrialization or educational norms?
3. **Measurement of Outcomes:** What comprehensive evaluation and feedback systems will you establish to regularly assess the effectiveness of TVET programs? How will these insights drive continuous improvement and responsiveness to both student needs and global industry trends?

5.1 Germany, The TVET MAESTRO

"This mastery is evident in Germany's approach to seamlessly *integrating technical and vocational education with real-world industry requirements."*

A maestro orchestrates with precision, ensuring every note aligns perfectly to create a symphony of excellence. In the realm of TVET, Germany performs as the Maestro, masterfully tuning its educational strategies to industry rhythms, fostering a workforce as skilled and harmonious as a finely-tuned orchestra. This adeptness in TVET not only shapes careers but also drives the nation's economic success.

This mastery is evident in Germany's approach to seamlessly integrating technical and vocational education with real-world industry requirements. The meticulous design of the TVET DUAL system ensures that every student receives education that is precisely aligned with current and future job markets, effectively preparing them for successful careers. This strategic alignment enhances Germany's global competitiveness by developing a highly skilled workforce ready to tackle technological advancements and complex industrial challenges.

The German TVET model, therefore, not only cultivates individual talent but also contributes significantly to the nation's broader economic landscape, proving itself as an exemplary leader in vocational training worldwide.

As the global landscape evolves, Germany continues to refine and adapt its TVET system, ensuring it remains at the forefront of educational excellence and economic innovation.

5.2 A TVET MASTERPIECE

"...a masterpiece of vocational education that harmoniously combined apprenticeships in industry with structured vocational schooling."

A Masterpiece indeed.

The modern TVET Dual System of vocational education and training in Germany was formally established in the 1960s.

However, the evolution of Germany's vocational training system is rooted much deeper in history, primarily beginning with the guild training system before transitioning to more structured formats. Post-World War II, Germany faced the imperative task of rebuilding its economy and workforce.

In response, the Dual System was born, a masterpiece of vocational education that harmoniously combined apprenticeships in industry with structured vocational schooling. This system was meticulously structured and regulated to ensure a high standard of education and training.

It bridged the gap between theoretical knowledge and practical application, a crucial element that was necessary to swiftly and effectively meet the modern needs of a recovering and rapidly industrializing nation. By coordinating education with real-world industrial requirements, the Dual System played a pivotal role in revitalizing Germany's economic engine, setting a global benchmark in vocational training.

Here's a table summarizing the progression from guilds to the modern Dual System, highlighting key phases and characteristics:

Era	Training System	Characteristics	Purpose and Evolution
Medieval Period	Guild Training	- Training was highly specialized and controlled by guilds. - Apprentices worked directly under master craftsmen.	- Focused on hands-on skills for specific trades. - Ensured high-quality craftsmanship and control over trade standards.
Industrial Revolution	Factory Schools	- Rise of factory-based training alongside emerging industries. - More formalized than guild training but less regulated.	- Aimed to quickly skill workers for specific factory tasks. - Addressed the growing demand for industrial labour.
Early 20th Century	School-based Vocational Education	- Formal vocational schools began to emerge. - Curricula were more standardized but less integrated with industry.	- Provided broader educational content. - Sought to expand accessibility to vocational training beyond traditional trades.
Post-WWII	Dual System	- Combines apprenticeships in industry with vocational schooling. - Highly structured and regulated.	- Bridges gap between theory and practice. - Meets modern industrial needs with coordinated education and training.

This evolution reflects Germany's response to changing economic and industrial demands, moving from the highly controlled guild system through more rudimentary factory training and school-based vocational education, culminating in the Dual System. Each stage built on the previous one, increasingly integrating practical experience with theoretical learning to adapt to technological advances and the needs of a growing economy.

Hence, in Germany's TVET landscape, the term "Dual" resonates like a well-composed duet between education and industry. This system uniquely weaves together rigorous academic instruction at vocational schools with hands-on apprenticeship experience within companies, creating a harmonious blend that expertly prepares students for the complexities of the modern workforce.

5.3 An "Orchestra" for TVET

> *"By conceptualizing the TVET system in this way, we can appreciate how each component plays a specific role, contributing to the overall effectiveness and harmony of the system."*

In order to see things differently, let's do this creatively.

Imagine a grand orchestral arrangement where each component synchronizes perfectly to create a symphony of excellence. This analogy captures the essence of Germany's renowned TVET system, particularly its Dual System, which exemplifies a harmonized interplay of various key elements. Let's explore this metaphor to understand how the components of the TVET system might be arranged if they were part of an orchestral layout.

1. **Strings (Industry and Company Involvement)**: Just as the string section forms the foundation of the

orchestra with its wide range of pitches and timbre diversity, industry and company involvement form the core of the TVET system. These entities drive the training process by setting the standards and expectations for skills and knowledge, much like how the strings often carry the melody and harmony in a musical piece.

2. **Woodwinds (Educational Institutions)**: Positioned strategically to blend with the strings, the educational institutions in the TVET system function like the woodwinds. They add depth and colour to the training provided by interpreting the industry's needs and translating them into comprehensive educational programs. Their role is essential in bridging the practical training provided by companies with theoretical knowledge, similar to how woodwinds often provide crucial counterpoints and lead passages in an orchestra.
3. **Brass (Governmental Support)**: The brass section provides power and strength in an orchestra, often emphasizing climactic points or foundational harmonies. In the TVET system, governmental support provides the necessary policies, funding, and regulatory frameworks that uphold the structure of the system. This support ensures the stability and efficacy of the training programs, much like how the brass solidifies the musical structure.
4. **Percussion (Regulatory and Certification Bodies)**: Just as percussion instruments add rhythm and highlight transitions within a musical piece, regulatory and certification bodies ensure that the TVET system meets its benchmarks and maintains quality. They provide the checks and balances that keep the system dynamic and responsive to changing economic and industrial landscapes.

By conceptualizing the TVET system in this way, we can appreciate how each component plays a specific role, contributing to the overall effectiveness and harmony of the system. Each part must function in concert with the others, just as each section of the orchestra must coordinate with the rest to create a compelling musical performance.

TVET360 has outlined The Maestro key "orchestral" components with clarity and examples, here is a detailed table:

Component	Role in TVET System	Examples
Strings (Industry and Company Involvement)	Drives the curriculum and provides practical training. Ensures skills are relevant to current industry needs.	Siemens AG partnering with vocational schools to provide hands-on training and apprenticeships in engineering.
Woodwinds (Educational Institutions)	Delivers tailored education that bridges practical training with theoretical knowledge.	The Technical University of Munich offering specialized courses in robotics that complement apprenticeships in manufacturing.
Brass (Governmental Support)	Provides the foundational support with policies, funding, and regulations.	German Federal Ministry of Education and Research funding innovative TVET programs in renewable energy technologies.
Percussion (Regulatory and Certification Bodies)	Ensures the system meets benchmarks and maintains quality. Provides checks and balances.	The German Chambers of Industry and Commerce (IHK) certifying vocational qualifications and overseeing training standards.

This table outlines how the orchestral sections metaphorically represent the integral components of the TVET system, each contributing to a harmonious and effective vocational education and training environment. These components work in concert to ensure that the system remains dynamic, responsive, and aligned with both current and future economic and industrial needs. The examples provided demonstrate the practical application of these roles within the system, highlighting the collaborative efforts that sustain and enhance the quality and relevance of vocational training in Germany.

5.4 The "Perfect" Audience

"Just as a maestro without an audience merely rehearses, the essence of TVET without its dedicated and diverse students lacks the resonance and impact of real-world application..."

Is there such a thing as The "Perfect" Audience?

To any Maestro, the 'perfect' audience is akin to the silent yet vital partner in the concert hall, whose deep appreciation and keen understanding of the music elevate the performance's spirit and execution. Just as a maestro without an audience merely rehearses, the essence of TVET without its dedicated and diverse students lacks the resonance and impact of real-world application, turning vibrant potential into unfulfilled echoes in an empty hall.

In Germany, the "perfect audience" for the TVET system comprises a diverse and dynamic demographic of students who opt for vocational training as a credible and rewarding educational pathway. Approximately 50% to 60% of secondary students in Germany enrol in the TVET system, drawn by its robust structure, strong industry connections, and clear career pathways. This high participation rate reflects the societal value placed on vocational education and its perceived efficacy in securing gainful employment.

TVET students typically range from teens aiming for direct professional entry to young adults enhancing their skills or retraining. They are characterized by:

- A practical mind-set motivated by hands-on learning.
- A desire to learn through real-world applications.
- The prospect of earning while learning through apprenticeships.

The system attracts both genders across sectors like manufacturing, IT, and healthcare. Germany's ability to maintain such a "perfect audience" is supported by:

- Strong societal recognition of vocational training's value.
- Substantial state support through funding and quality control.
- Active industry involvement in curriculum development and training.

Germany's success in maintaining such a "perfect audience" is also supported by the strong societal recognition of vocational training's value, substantial support from the state in terms of funding and quality control, and the active involvement of companies in shaping curricula and providing training placements. This multifaceted support ensures that TVET is not seen as a lesser choice but as a different, yet equally prestigious, educational pathway.

Next, we will explore examples of these "perfect audiences" and their journeys through the Dual System.

Note: This section specifically addresses fresh students, primarily around the age of 15, who are transitioning from the school system into TVET programs. It is important to recognize that TVET also supports a broader agenda of lifelong learning, catering to a diverse range of students and professionals seeking continuous skill development throughout their careers.

However, that is not with our scope.

5.5 The Two 'SHOWS' of DUAL

> *"These are the only available routes in Germany's TVET system, making them consistent, reliable, and clear for both students and employers."*

Germany's Technical and Vocational Education and Training (TVET) system offers two main routes to accommodate different career goals:

The Traditional Vocational Route and the Advanced Vocational Route.

A) Traditional Vocational Route (TVR)

Traditional Vocational Route*: Focuses on apprenticeships and company-based training, targeting direct skill acquisition for immediate job readiness in various industries.

- **Venue:** Combines vocational school theory with practical company training.

- **Duration:** Typically lasts 2 to 3.5 years, depending on the trade.

*Note: Students can attend basic skill schools or similar vocational programs **before** entering an apprenticeship, but it is **not a requirement** for the **Traditional Vocational Route** in Germany. Many students choose to start their apprenticeship directly after completing general secondary education, while others may seek **pre-apprenticeship training** or attend a **basic vocational school** (such as a culinary school) to build foundational skills in their chosen field.

Hence, within the Traditional Vocational Route (TVR) there are two Possible Pathways:

(TVR1) Direct Apprenticeship**:** Most students enter apprenticeships right after secondary school, without prior specialized training. The vocational school and company-based training during the apprenticeship will provide the necessary culinary skills for those training to be bakers, chefs, etc.

(TVR2) Pre-Apprenticeship or Vocational School**:** Some students may choose to attend a basic vocational program or culinary school before beginning an apprenticeship to gain some foundational skills. This can give them an advantage during the apprenticeship application process, as they may already have some relevant knowledge or practical experience.

Also within the Advanced Vocational Route (AVR) there are two Possible Pathways:

In the Advanced Vocational Route (AVR), particularly in the Technical Education path at Universities of Applied Sciences, internships play a significant role. Here's how internships fit into the two paths:

(AVR1) Meister Route:

- Internships are generally not required in the Meister Route. The focus here is on specialized vocational training and mastery of a trade, often building on previous practical experience gained through an apprenticeship.
- The hands-on component in the Meister Route comes more from advanced training at vocational schools and industry chambers rather than through internships.

(AVR 2) Technical Education at Universities of Applied Sciences:

- **Internships are commonly integrated** into the curriculum for bachelor's or master's degrees at Universities of Applied Sciences. These internships provide practical experience in technical or managerial roles, complementing the theoretical education.
- **Structure**: Students often complete **mandatory internships** during their degree programs, typically lasting a few months, to gain real-world experience in their field of study.
- **Goal**: Internships help students apply the skills and knowledge they've acquired in class to practical, work-based scenarios, preparing them for the labor market. These internships are crucial for bridging academic learning with industry practices.

Summary of Pathways:

Dual Pathways	Types	Format
Traditional Vocational Route (TVR)	TVR1	Direct Apprenticeship
	TVR2	Pre-Apprenticeship
Advanced Vocational Route (AVR)	AVR1	Meister
	AVR2	Technical Education

The importance of Germany's two TVET routes, the Traditional Vocational Route (TVR) and Advanced Vocational Route (AVR), lies in their flexibility, transparency, and alignment with diverse career goals and industry needs. These are the only available routes in Germany's TVET system, making them consistent, reliable, and clear for both students and employers.

The TVR focuses on hands-on apprenticeships, enabling students to gain practical skills directly in the workplace, ensuring immediate job readiness. This pathway benefits industries that require skilled workers quickly, and it provides students a direct transition from education to employment.

The AVR emphasizes advanced specialization through technical education, preparing students for higher-level roles in management or technical fields. This route supports innovation and industry leadership, offering opportunities for lifelong learning and career advancement, particularly through programs like the Meister certification or internships at Universities of Applied Sciences.

Together, these two transparent and structured routes ensure a dynamic workforce that meets both immediate labor market needs and the demand for highly skilled professionals in an evolving economy.

Next, let's see how the pathways are being deployed by some fictional students.

5.5.1 Hans, a Graphic Designer

Journey for Hans: Becoming a Graphic Designer

Introducing an "Audience" named Hans.

Hans is 15 years of age and dreams of being a successful Graphic Designer.

He has chosen the DUAL TVET pathway to embark on.

In Germany's dual TVET system, becoming a graphic designer involves a 2-3 year apprenticeship where learners split their time between vocational school and hands-on training in a design studio or company. At school, they study design principles, typography, color theory, and digital tools like Adobe Creative Suite. They also learn about client communication, project management, and marketing strategies. In the workplace, they gain practical experience by working on real-world projects, such as designing logos, brochures, websites, and other visual materials. A graphic designer is responsible for creating visual content that communicates messages effectively, ensuring it meets client needs and industry standards.

Maya has prepared this tables that outlines both the Traditional Vocational Route an (TVR2) and the Advanced Vocational Route, including details about the duration of each stage, wages during and after completion, along with an explanation of what Hans can expect at each stage:

<u>> Traditional Pre-Apprenticeship Path Table for Hans: Becoming a Graphic Designer (TVR2)</u>

MAYA® ChatGPT

Stage	Venue	Duration	Years to Complete	Explanation	Expected Wages
Basic Design Principles	Vocational and Technical School (Design Institute)	1 year	1	Hans begins with foundational education in graphic design, learning about color theory, typography, and basic design principles.	None (Study Phase)
Apprenticeship	Design Studio or Agency	1 year	2	Hans applies his design skills in a real-world setting, working in design studios or advertising agencies.	$20,000 - $30,000 annually (Internship)
Professional Certification	Design Certification Center	Immediate after internship	2	Hans obtains his professional certification, validating his skills and readiness to work in professional design settings.	Upon Certification: $35,000 - $45,000 annually
Employment / Entrepreneurial	Various Venues	Career-long	Career-long	Equipped with practical experience and certification, Hans is ready for employment or to venture into his own design business.	$45,000 - $60,000 annually; varies with experience and location

Total Years Required to Complete Traditional Path: <u>Minimum 2 years</u>

<u>> Advanced Vocational Path Table for Hans: Becoming a Graphic Designer (AVR2)</u>

MAYA® ChatGPT

Stage	Venue	Duration	Years to Complete	Explanation	Expected Wages
Basic Design Principles	Vocational and Technical School (Design Institute)	1 year	1	Starts with foundational graphic design skills, essential for any designer.	None (Study Phase)
Advanced Design Techniques	Specialized Design School	1 year	2	Pursues advanced studies focusing on digital design, UX/UI design, and multimedia art.	$25,000 - $35,000 annually (Advanced Study Phase)
Specialization	Specialized Design School	1 year	3	Chooses a specialization such as web design, animation, or branding to master a particular design niche.	Upon Specialization: $40,000 - $50,000 annually
Leadership and Management Training	Business School or Leadership Institute	1 year	4	Studies aspects of design management and leadership to prepare for roles such as art director or creative manager.	Upon Training: $55,000 - $70,000 annually
Employment / Entrepreneurial	Various Venues	Career-long	Career-long	With a blend of advanced training and specialized skills, Hans is well-prepared for leadership roles in design settings or his own business.	$70,000+ annually; varies significantly with role and experience

Total Years Required to Complete Advanced Path: 4 years

This wages section outlines the estimated earnings Hans might expect during his studies, internships, and professional career, providing a realistic financial perspective of pursuing a career in graphic design through both the Traditional and Advanced paths.

5.5.2 Gwen, a Baker

Journey for Gwen: Becoming a Baker

Introducing an "Audience" named Gwen.

Gwen is 15 years of age and dreams of being a successful Baker. She has chosen the DUAL TVET pathway to embark on.

In Germany's dual TVET system, becoming a baker involves a comprehensive apprenticeship lasting 2-3 years, where apprentices split their time between vocational school and practical, on-the-job training in a bakery. At school, they study the science of baking, including dough preparation, fermentation, and ingredient selection, while also learning about hygiene standards, bakery management, and customer service. In the bakery, they apply these skills, gaining hands-on experience in producing bread, pastries, cakes, and other baked goods. A baker is responsible for maintaining product quality, ensuring cleanliness, and working efficiently in either commercial or artisan settings to meet customer demand.

Maya has prepared this table that outlines both the Traditional Vocational Route and the Advanced Vocational Route, including details about the duration of each stage, wages during and after completion, along with an explanation of what Gwen can expect at each stage:

>Traditional (Pre-Apprenticeship-TVR2) Path Table for Gwen: Becoming a Baker

MAYA@ ChatGPT

Stage	Venue	Duration	Years to Complete	Explanation	Expected Wages
Basic Baking Skills	Vocational and Technical School (Culinary School)	1 year	1	Gwen begins her education focusing on fundamental baking techniques, ingredient knowledge, and kitchen safety.	None (Study Phase)
Apprenticeship	Bakery	2 years	3	Applies her skills in a real-world setting, working in a bakery to gain hands-on experience with various pastries.	\$20,000-\$25,000 annually (Apprentice)
Professional Certification	Culinary Institute	Immediate after apprenticeship	3	Obtains professional baking certification, validating her skills and readiness to work in professional settings.	Upon Certification: \$30,000-\$35,000 annually
Employment/ Entrepreneurial	Various Bakeries	Career-long	Career-long	Equipped with practical experience and certification, Gwen is ready for employment or to open her own bakery.	\$35,000-\$45,000 annually; varies with experience and location

TVET 360

Total Years Required to Complete Traditional Path: Minimum 6 years

> Advanced Vocational Path Table for Gwen: Becoming a Baker

MAYA@ ChatGPT

Stage	Venue	Duration	Years to Complete	Explanation	Expected Wages
Basic Baking Skills	Vocational and Technical School (Culinary School)	1 year	1	Starts with foundational skills essential for any professional baker.	None (Study Phase)
Advanced Baking Techniques	Specialized Baking Academy	2 years	3	Pursues advanced studies focusing on artisan breads, pastries, and international baking styles.	$25,000 - $30,000 annually (Advanced Study Phase)
Specialization	Specialized Baking Academy	1 year	4	Chooses a specialization such as artisan bread making, pastry arts, or dietary-specific baking.	Upon Specialization: $40,000 - $45,000 annually
Leadership and Management Training	Business School	1 year	5	Studies business management, food safety laws, and customer service to prepare for roles such as bakery manager or owner.	Upon Training: $50,000 - $60,000 annually
Employment/ Entrepreneurial	Various Bakeries	Career-long	Career-long	With advanced training and specialized skills, Gwen is well-prepared for leadership roles or to run her own bakery.	$60,000+ annually; varies significantly with role and experience

TVET 360

Total Years Required to Complete Advanced Path: min 5 years

Each table outlines Gwen's structured progression through both traditional and advanced baking education and training, aligning her career aspirations directly with practical and managerial roles in the baking industry.

5.5.3. Ericsson, an Electrical Engineer

Introducing an "Audience" named Ericsson.

Journey for Ericsson: Becoming an Electrical Engineer

Ericsson is 15 years of age and dreams of being a successful Electrical Engineer. He has chosen the DUAL TVET pathway to embark on.

Germany's dual TVET system, there is indeed a pathway where someone can begin their journey to becoming an electrical engineer through an apprenticeship. This pathway typically starts with an apprenticeship as an electrical technician, lasting 3-4 years, where learners split their time between vocational school and practical work at a company. During this apprenticeship, students focus on electrical installations, maintenance, and repair of electrical systems, learning hands-on skills in wiring, troubleshooting, and using electrical tools. After completing the apprenticeship, individuals can either enter the workforce as qualified technicians or pursue further studies—such as attending a university of applied sciences to obtain a bachelor's degree in electrical engineering. This pathway allows for a practical foundation in the field, followed by advanced education and theoretical knowledge, ultimately leading to a career as a professional electrical engineer.

> Traditional Apprenticeship Path Table for Ericsson: Becoming an Electrical Engineer (TVR1)

Stage	Venue	Duration	Years to Complete	Explanation	Expected Wages
Direct Apprenticeship	Engineering Firm	3-4 years	3-4 years	The student enters directly into an engineering apprenticeship, gaining practical, hands-on experience while working on projects under the guidance of engineers.	$30,000 - $45,000 annually (Apprentice)
Journey-man Engineer	Engineering Certification Board	Upon completion	3-4 years	Upon completing the apprenticeship, the student becomes a Journeyman, gaining basic certifications and readiness to work independently in limited engineering roles.	$50,000 - $70,000 annually
Advanced Certification	Engineering Licensing Board	Career-long	Varies	With further work experience, the apprentice pursues advanced certifications and licensure exams to become a fully licensed Professional Engineer (PE).	$70,000 - $100,000 annually
Employment/Entrepreneurial	Various Engineering Firms or Consulting Firms	Career-long	Career-long	After obtaining full licensure and practical experience, the individual is prepared for advanced positions or self-employment through consulting.	$80,000 - $120,000 annually

The total number of years to become a fully licensed Professional Engineer (PE) through this pathway would be approximately 7-9 years:

- Apprenticeship (3-4 years)
- Additional work experience (4-5 years) to qualify for advanced certification and licensing exams.

This pathway allows students to bypass formal academic education and instead focus on learning through practical work, gaining the necessary qualifications over time through certifications and licensing exams.

>Traditional Pre-Apprenticeship Path Table for Ericsson: Becoming an Electrical Engineer (TVR2)

Stage	Venue	Duration	Years to Complete	Explanation	Expected Wages
Pre-Apprenticeship Program	Vocational and Technical School	6 months - 1 year	0.5 - 1 year	Provides foundational knowledge in electrical systems, basic wiring, blueprint reading, and safety protocols to prepare for the apprenticeship.	None (Study Phase)
Apprenticeship (Electrical Focus)	Electrical Engineering Firm	3-4 years	3-4 years	Hands-on training under licensed electrical engineers, gaining practical experience in electrical systems, wiring, power distribution, and maintenance.	$30,000 - $45,000 annually (Apprentice)
Journeyman Electrician/ Engineer	Engineering Certification Board	Upon completion	3-4 years	After completing the apprenticeship, the individual becomes a certified Journeyman, qualified to work on electrical systems under limited supervision.	$50,000 - $70,000 annually
Professional Certification	Electrical Licensing Board	Career-long	Varies	With further experience, the electrical engineer pursues advanced certification and licensure, becoming a fully licensed Professional Electrical Engineer.	$70,000 - $100,000 annually
Employment/Entrepreneurial	Electrical Engineering Firms/Consultancy	Career-long	Career-long	After obtaining full licensure and years of experience, the individual is ready for employment in high-level positions or starting an electrical consultancy.	$80,000 - $120,000 annually

Total Number of Years:

- Pre-Apprenticeship: 0.5 - 1 year
- Apprenticeship: 3-4 years
- Additional Work Experience (for full licensure): 4-5 years

Total Years Needed: 7.5 - 10 years to become a fully licensed Professional Electrical Engineer.

5.5.4. Leon, a Media Designer

Introducing an "Audience" named Leon.

Journey for Leon: Becoming a Media Designer

Leon is 15 years of age and dreams of being a successful Media Designer. He has chosen the DUAL TVET pathway to embark on.

Media designers are responsible for producing visually engaging and effective multimedia content for advertising, entertainment, or corporate communications, ensuring it aligns with client needs and industry standards. Upon completion, graduates are well-prepared for the creative media industry.

In Germany, becoming a media designer can be pursued through both the apprenticeship route and the advanced vocational route. The 3-year apprenticeship involves splitting time between vocational school and hands-on training in a media company, where students gain practical experience in graphic design, video production, and web development. Alternatively, the advanced vocational route allows students to further their education at a University of Applied Sciences, leading to a bachelor's degree in media design or related fields. This route offers specialization in advanced design techniques and digital media, preparing individuals for managerial roles or more complex creative projects. Both pathways provide strong career foundations.

Maya has prepared this table that outlines both the Traditional Vocational Route and the Advanced Vocational Route, including details about the duration of each stage, wages during and after completion, along with an explanation of what Hans can expect at each stage:

>Traditional Vocational Route (AVR1) Table for Leon: Becoming a Media Designer

MAYA@ ChatGPT

Stage	Venue	Duration	Years to Complete	Explanation	Expected Wages
Basic Media Design Principles	Vocational and Technical School (Design School)	1 year	1	Leon begins his education with foundational training in graphic design, video production, and web design.	None (Study Phase)
Apprenticeship	Media Studio or Advertising Agency	1 year	2	Applies his skills in a real-world setting, working on projects that involve creating visual content for various media.	$25,000 - $30,000 annually (Intern)
Professional Certification	Media Design Certification Body	Immediate after internship	2	Obtains a professional certification, validating his skills and readiness to work in professional media design settings.	Upon Certification: $40,000 - $50,000 annually
Employment/ Entrepreneurial	Various Media Studios or Freelance	Career-long	Career-long	Equipped with practical experience and certification, Leon is ready for employment or to freelance in media design.	$50,000 - $60,000 annually; varies with experience and location

Total Years Required to Complete via a Traditional Vocational Route: Minimum 4 years (TVR1)

> Advanced Vocational Route for Leon: Becoming a Media Designer (AVR2)

MAYA@ ChatGPT

Stage	Venue	Duration	Years to Complete	Explanation	Expected Wages
Basic Media Design Principles	Vocational and Technical School (Design School)	1 year	1	Begins with fundamental skills essential for any professional media designer.	None (Study Phase)
Advanced Media Concepts	Specialized Design Institute	2 years	3	Pursues advanced studies focusing on emerging media technologies, interactive design, and multimedia storytelling.	$30,000 - $35,000 annually (Advanced Study Phase)
Specialization	Specialized Design Institute or Workshop	1 year	4	Specializes in a niche area such as animation, UX/UI design, or digital marketing to master a particular design focus.	Upon Specialization: $55,000 - $65,000 annually
Leadership and Management Training	Business School or Leadership Institute	1 year	5	Studies project management, creative direction, and business aspects of design firms.	Upon Training: $70,000 - $80,000 annually
Employment/ Entrepreneurial	Various Media Studios or Freelance	Career-long	Career-long	With advanced training and specialized skills, Leon is well-prepared for leadership roles or to run his own design studio.	$80,000+ annually; varies significantly with role and experience

Total Years Required to Complete Advanced Path: Minimum 5 years

Each table provides a structured progression through both traditional and advanced media design education and training, aligning Leon's career aspirations directly with practical and managerial roles in the media design industry. These pathway provides a structured approach for Leon from education through to professional development, aligning his training with real-world applications in the field of media design within Germany's TVET system.

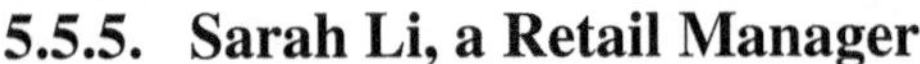

5.5.5. Sarah Li, a Retail Manager

Introducing an "Audience" named Sarah Li.

Journey for Sarah Li: Becoming a Retail Sales Manager

Sarah Li is 15 years of age and dreams of being a successful Retail Sales Manager. She has chosen the DUAL TVET pathway to embark on.

In Germany, becoming a Retail Sales Manager can be pursued through both the apprenticeship route and the advanced vocational route. The apprenticeship typically lasts 2-3 years, combining vocational school education with practical experience in a retail setting, where students learn customer service, sales techniques, inventory management, and retail operations. The advanced vocational route allows individuals to further their education at a University of Applied Sciences or specialized vocational schools, leading to a bachelor's degree or Meisterbrief, focusing on advanced management skills, business strategies, and leadership. Both pathways equip learners with the skills needed for success in retail management roles.

A Retail Sales Manager's job includes overseeing day-to-day store operations, managing staff, driving sales, optimizing inventory, ensuring customer satisfaction, and meeting financial targets to support business growth.

Maya has prepared this table that outlines both the Traditional Vocational Route and the Advanced Vocational Route, including details about the duration of each stage, wages during and after completion, along with an explanation of what Sarah can expect at each stage:

<u>>Traditional Path Table for Sarah Li: Becoming a Retail Sales Manager</u>

MAYA@ ChatGPT

Stage	Venue	Duration	Years to Complete	Explanation	Expected Wages
Retail Basics and Sales Techniques	Vocational/Technical School {Local Retail Training Centre}	1 year	1	Sarah begins her education in retail, learning basic sales techniques, customer service, and store operations.	None {Study Phase}
On-the-Job Training	Retail Store	1 year	2	Applies her skills in a real-world retail setting, working directly with customers and dealing with daily store management tasks.	$25,000 - $30,000 annually {Trainee}
Professional Certification	Retail Management Institute	Immediate after training	2	Obtains a certification in retail management, which validates her ability to handle managerial responsibilities in retail settings.	Upon Certification: $35,000 - $40,000 annually
Employment/ Entrepreneurial	Various Retail Venues	Career-long	Career-long	With practical experience and certification, Sarah is prepared for employment or to manage her own retail business.	$40,000 - $55,000 annually; varies with experience and location

Total Years Required to Complete Traditional Path: <u>Minimum 4 years</u>

>Advanced Path Table for Sarah Li: Becoming a Retail Sales Manager (AVR2)

Stage	Venue	Duration	Years to Complete	Explanation	Expected Wages
Bachelor's in Retail Management	University of Applied Sciences	Full-time program	3-4 years	Comprehensive study of retail management, customer relations, marketing, business operations, and supply chain management, with internships for practical experience.	$40,000–$50,000 annually upon completion
Master's in Business Management (optional)	University of Applied Sciences	Full-time program	1-2 years	Specializes in advanced business management, leadership skills, financial planning, and strategic decision-making for senior retail roles.	$50,000–$65,000 annually upon completion
Internship/ Co-op Programs	Partner Retail Companies	Integrated within degree	Part of degree program	Provides hands-on work experience in retail operations, customer service, and business strategy as part of the applied university curriculum.	Internship wages, varies
Advanced Retail Strategy and Leadership	University of Applied Sciences	6 months – 1 year	Optional after Bachelor's or Master's	Further specialization in retail strategy, innovation, entrepreneurship, and leadership training, often for high-level or entrepreneurial roles.	$55,000–$70,000 annually upon completion
Career Entry / Employment	Various Retail Companies or Self-Employment	Career-long	-	Graduates enter retail management roles in businesses or pursue entrepreneurial ventures, with potential for career growth through experience and ongoing professional development.	$60,000–$80,000 annually, varies with experience

Total Years Required to Complete Advanced Path: Minimum 5 years

This framework above provides Sarah with a structured progression through both traditional and advanced retail management education and training, aligning her career aspirations directly with practical and managerial roles in the retail industry.

5.5.6. Lara, an Architect

Introducing an "Audience" named Lara.

Journey for Lara: Becoming an Architect

Lara is 15 years of age and dreams of being a successful Architect. She has chosen the DUAL TVET pathway to embark on.

In Germany, becoming an **Architect** can be pursued through both the **apprenticeship route** and the **advanced vocational route**. The apprenticeship typically lasts 2-3 years, combining vocational school education with practical experience in an architectural firm, where students learn basic architectural design, construction methods, and project management. The advanced vocational route allows individuals to further their education at a **University of Applied Sciences** or **Meister school**, leading to a **Meisterbrief** or bachelor's degree, with a focus on advanced architectural techniques, project planning, and leadership.

Both pathways equip learners with the skills needed for success in architectural roles.

An **Architect's job** includes designing buildings, planning construction projects, managing teams, ensuring compliance with regulations, and delivering aesthetically pleasing and functional structures that meet client needs and industry standards. Architects also manage budgets, timelines, and collaborate with engineers and construction teams to ensure projects are completed efficiently and effectively.

Maya has prepared this table that outlines the Advanced Vocational Route, including details about the duration of each stage, wages during and after completion, along with an explanation of what Lara can expect at each stage:

>Advanced Vocational Route for Lara: Becoming an Architect (AVR1):

Stage	Venue	Duration	Years to Complete	Explanation	Expected Wages
Basic Architectural Principles	Technical and Vocational School	2-3 years	2-3 years	Covers foundational skills in architectural design, construction methods, and building materials.	$30,000 - $40,000 (upon completion)
Apprenticeship in Architecture	Architectural Firm/Industry Partners	2-3 years	2-3 years	Combines vocational schooling with hands-on architectural work, focusing on drafting, design, and construction.	$35,000 - $50,000 (upon completion)
Meister Certification in Architecture	Meister School/Chamber of Crafts	1-2 years	1-2 years	Focuses on advanced architectural techniques, project management, and leadership to achieve Meister status.	$55,000 - $70,000 (upon completion)
Leadership and Project Management	Meister School or Business Institute	1 year	1 year	Develops skills in leading architectural projects, managing teams, and business administration.	$70,000 - $80,000 (after certification)
Employment/Entrepreneurship	Architectural Firms/Own Business	Career-long	-	Opportunities to manage architectural projects, lead design teams, or start an independent practice as a certified Meister.	$80,000+ (varies with experience)

Total Years Required to Complete Advanced Vocational Route (AVR1) : 6-9 years

This table outlines **Lara's pathway** through a **Meister TVET program** in **Architecture**, focusing on technical skills, practical experience, advanced certification, and leadership training. After completing the Meister certification, she can manage projects or run her own architectural firm.

5.6 The DUAL Encore

> *"This structure is crucial because it provides predictability and reliability, ensuring that learners understand their career options from the outset."*

What makes them come back for more, how is the DUAL so sustainable?

The dual system's effectiveness in maintaining low youth unemployment rates in Germany can be attributed to several key factors that make it highly attractive and beneficial for young individuals. Primarily, the system's structured approach to education, which combines theoretical learning with practical application, ensures that students are not only knowledgeable but also skilled in ways that are directly applicable to the job market. This dual approach reduces the skill gap often faced by graduates of more traditional educational systems.

Key Attractions of Germany's Dual System

1. Practical Skill Acquisition: Combines theoretical learning with practical application, directly addressing the skills gap.
2. Direct Industry Involvement: Curriculum tailored by industry partnerships, ensuring relevance and high employability.
3. Financial Incentives During Training: Apprentices earn wages, providing financial stability and incentive to complete training.

a) Overview of the German Traditional Vocational Education System:

This is how Hans and his friends above would progress through the DUAL environment, it begins with:

- Age of Decision: At around 15 or 16, students choose to pursue vocational training based on interests and academic performance.
- Choosing a Vocational School: Students select schools specialized in their career interests, aligning education with specific industry needs.
- Apprenticeship: Students must secure an apprenticeship to gain hands-on experience, integrating school learning with real-world application.
- Dual System: Education splits between vocational school and workplace, blending theory and practice for comprehensive skill development.
- Further Progression: Post-training, options include advanced vocational training or academic advancement at universities of applied sciences.

Common Training Experience:

- All students, irrespective of their field (e.g., media design, baking, retail management), undergo a similar foundational process:

- Choice of Specialization: Selection of a vocational school tailored to their field.
- Apprenticeship Matching: Securing an apprenticeship that complements their studies.
- Dual Education: Engaging in both classroom and on-the-job training.

This structured approach not only prepares students effectively for the job market by providing relevant skills but also supports their financial needs during training, making vocational education a compelling alternative to traditional academic pathways.

b) Overview of the Advanced Technical Pathway:

- Continuation After Initial Training: Typically follows the completion of an initial vocational qualification or several years of work experience.
- Enrollment in Technikerschulen or Fachschulen: Students enroll in schools offering advanced technical training (Technikerschule) or specialize in certain professions (Fachschule), providing advanced knowledge and skills.
- Curriculum Focus: The curriculum includes advanced technical skills, industry-specific technologies, and management training.
- Duration: Programs generally last 2-3 years, providing comprehensive expertise and management skills.
- Certifications and Degrees: Successful completion can lead to higher diplomas, state-certified technician or specialist qualifications, which are highly respected in the industry.

So what does this mean?

Dual Pathways	Types	Format
Traditional Vocational Route (TVR)	**TVR1**	**Direct Apprenticeship**
	TVR2	**Pre-Apprenticeship**
Advanced Vocational Route (AVR)	**AVR1**	**Meister**
	AVR2	**Technical Education**

The table highlights Germany's dual pathways into TVET: the Traditional Vocational Route (TVR) and the Advanced Vocational Route (AVR). TVR includes direct apprenticeships (TVR1) and pre-apprenticeships (TVR2), providing hands-on skills early on. AVR offers two advanced options: Meister certification (AVR1) for mastery in a trade and technical education (AVR2) for specialized knowledge.

Germany's TVET system ensures clear, transparent pathways for learners, allowing them to navigate their career paths efficiently from apprenticeship to advanced qualifications. This structure is crucial because it provides predictability and reliability, ensuring that learners understand their career options from the outset. It helps match training with industry needs, creating a skilled workforce aligned with labor market demands. Additionally, this clarity boosts employer confidence, knowing that graduates have undergone standardized, high-quality training. The system also offers flexibility, allowing learners to advance from technical roles to higher positions or further studies, enhancing career mobility and long-term professional growth.

5.7: Chapter 5 - Take-Away

Your Take-Away is ready!

The TVET Maestro focuses on Germany's dual TVET system, which is designed to provide various career pathways, including for vocations traditionally achieved through academic routes, such as architecture and engineering. This chapter highlights the flexibility of the dual system, ensuring that every vocation, from the trades to highly technical professions, has a structured and effective educational pathway.

In Germany, the popularity of the dual system is supported by a strong collaboration among government, industries, and educational institutions, which together ensure that the curricula remain current and closely tied to market needs. This close integration is crucial in maintaining low youth unemployment rates and in fostering a highly skilled workforce.

However, the chapter also implies that the unique socioeconomic and industrial context of Germany is a critical factor in the success of the dual system. The system's reliance on strong government support and active industry involvement may limit its applicability in countries with different economic structures or less coordinated industry-government relations. Thus, while highly successful in Germany, the dual system's model may not be easily replicable in other contexts without adaptations to local conditions.

Recommendations for TVET Policy Makers and Strategy Planners:

1. Strong Government and Legislative Support: Establish a solid legislative framework to support and safeguard TVET programs. Ensuring legal protection is vital for the sustainability and robustness of vocational training systems.
2. Adaptation to Local Contexts: Customize elements of the German dual system to fit specific local socioeconomic and industrial needs, identifying key industries for apprenticeships and adapting curricula accordingly.
3. Strengthen Industry-Education Partnerships: Enhance collaborations between educational institutions and industries. Build strong networks and partnerships with local businesses to keep TVET programs relevant and responsive. Offer incentives to encourage business participation.
4. Government Support and Incentives: Promote strong government support including funding, regulatory backing, and promotional efforts to enhance the quality and alignment of TVET programs with national economic objectives.
5. Implementing Clear Pathways and Outcomes: Develop distinct progression routes within TVET programs that clearly lead to certification, employment, or further education, helping students understand potential career trajectories.
6. Evaluation and Feedback Mechanisms: Establish systems for continuous evaluation and feedback involving all stakeholders, such as students, educators, and industry partners, to ensure ongoing improvement of the TVET system.

These recommendations are designed to streamline TVET systems, ensuring they are adaptive, well-supported, and effectively integrated with industry needs, thereby enhancing the relevance and efficiency of vocational training.

By implementing these strategies, TVET policy makers and planners can enhance the effectiveness of vocational education and training programs, making them more adaptable, relevant, and supportive of students and industries alike.

A TVET 360 STORY

Bonus: A TVET360 Story

(The story of South Korea's and India's TVET progress is exemplary. Here is a tale that tries to encapsulate their journey).

Train to Kuala Lumpur: A TVET TALE

Kumari-Devi, a bright and determined girl from a small village near Bangalore, sat by the window, watching the lush Malaysian countryside blur past. Each mile brought her closer to Kuala Lumpur, and her mind wandered back to her village. She remembered the early mornings filled with the crowing of roosters and the laughter of her late Amma, who believed in a better future for her. She always dreamt of becoming an engineer, but her family's financial struggles made higher education seem out of reach. Everything changed when she learned about the Industrial Training Institutes (ITIs) through a government outreach program.

India, gaining independence in 1947. It faced immense challenges as a newly sovereign state with deep-seated poverty and a largely agrarian economy. India launched the Skill India Mission in 2015, aiming to train over 400 million people by 2022. India's major industrial players like Tata, Infosys, and Larsen & Toubro have established robust vocational training programs that align with industry needs, ensuring that graduates are job-ready. India has seen a proliferation of Industrial Training Institutes (ITIs) and polytechnics, especially in rural and underserved areas, providing greater access to vocational education.

On the same train, Haneul-Dae, a good-looking Korean man, was similarly lost in thought. The sight of KL reminded him of the South Korean countryside, now replaced by Seoul's urban sprawl. He spent countless hours helping his father in their workshop. Growing up in a post-war economy, his family emphasized the importance of technical skills. Inspired by the success of chaebols like Samsung and Hyundai, he enrolled in a specialized high school with a comprehensive TVET curriculum, eventually ending up in vocational training.

South Korea emerged from the devastation of the Korean War in the 1950s with a shattered economy. South Korea initiated its transformation with the Vocational Training Promotion Act of 1967, which established a structured TVET framework. In South Korea, large conglomerates, or chaebols, such as Samsung, Hyundai, and LG, have played a critical role in the TVET landscape. These companies offer comprehensive apprenticeship programs that combine theoretical and practical training. South Korea has expanded its TVET system through specialized high schools, junior colleges, and polytechnics, focusing on advanced technologies and innovation.

Both nations recognized the urgent need to build a skilled workforce to drive economic growth and began laying the groundwork for comprehensive TVET systems. They have shown a strong commitment to integrating vocational training into their national development plans, fostering lifelong learning, and ensuring continuous skill development.

Both countries emphasize integrating cutting-edge technologies and innovative practices into their TVET programs.

As the train sped on, carrying both of them towards a new chapter, Kumari and Haneul reflected on their countries' progress. The

Indian government's Skill India Mission and South Korea's Vocational Training Promotion Act laid the foundation for their success. Kumari's internship at Tata Motors and Haneul's stint at Hyundai exemplified this synergy. Embracing lifelong learning, Kumari upgraded her skills through online courses, while Haneul pursued further certifications. Today, Kumari is a respected technician in Bangalore, inspiring many young girls to pursue vocational training. Haneul-Dae, now a skilled engineer at a top South Korean firm, shares his story with future TVET students, highlighting the opportunities TVET unlocked for him.

They arrived at KL Sentral. As passengers gathered their belongings, Kumari and Haneul-Dae rose from their seats, each lost in their thoughts. They bumped into each other in the aisle.

"Sorry!" Kumari said, smiling.

"No problem at all," Haneul replied, returning the smile.

They both laughed, easing the awkwardness. Walking toward the exit, they struck up a conversation.

"So, what brings you to Kuala Lumpur?" Kumari asked.

"I'm here for the Global TVET Conference," Haneul said. "And you?"

"Same here!" Kumari responded, beaming with pride. "I represent India. It's exciting to be part of something so significant."

As they walked through the bustling station, they shared their backgrounds. Kumari spoke of her journey from a small village to becoming a respected technician. Haneul-Dae recounted his experience at a vocational high school and his apprenticeship at LG. They found common ground in their struggles and triumphs.

At the station entrance, they bid each other goodbye.

"See you at the conference?" Kumari said.

"Definitely. Looking forward to it," Haneul replied.

Neither knew they would be key speakers.

The next morning, the conference began. A nervous Kumari-Devi walked into the main hall, surprised to see Haneul on the stage. He looked equally astonished. His smile was a welcoming sight for her.

"Welcome to our panel discussion," the moderator announced. "Today, we have two exemplary representatives from India and South Korea: Kumari-Devi and Haneul-Dae." The audience applauded as their backgrounds were read out.

The panel discussion began. Kumari shared her story, emphasizing the impact of the Skill India Mission on her life. She described her time at the ITI and her transformative internship at Tata Motors. Haneul-Dae followed, detailing South Korea's Vocational Training Promotion Act. He spoke about his apprenticeship at LG and how it shaped his career.

"Your journey is truly inspiring, Kumari," Haneul said during the discussion.

"And yours as well, Haneul-Dae," Kumari replied. "It's incredible how TVET has changed our lives."

During the Q&A session, someone asked, "What was the most profound change your country has made?"

Kumari-Devi thought for a moment. "For India, it's the empowerment of individuals through skills training. It's not just about jobs; it's about dignity and self-reliance."

Haneul-Dae nodded. "In South Korea, it's the integration of vocational training with industry needs. This alignment has driven innovation and economic growth."

South Korea promotes continuous skill development through policies that encourage workers to upgrade their skills regularly. India has adopted similar policies to ensure its workforce remains competitive in the global market. This commitment to lifelong learning has been crucial in maintaining economic adaptability and growth in both countries.

Today, both South Korea and India are recognized globally for their highly skilled workforces. South Korean professionals are renowned for their technical expertise in high-tech industries, while Indian professionals are celebrated for their versatility and innovative skills in various sectors. The TVET graduates from both nations contribute significantly to their domestic economies and are highly sought after internationally.

At lunch, Kumari and Haneul didn't sit together, but their eyes met across the room. Each reflected on the other's story, wondering if they would meet again to enjoy each other's company and stories.

Two years later, they did. Fate brought them together at another international conference. As soon as Kumari and Haneul saw each other, they knew their connection was special.

"Kumari!" Haneul-Dae called out.

"Hey, Haneul, it's been too long," she responded, smiling warmly.

As the theme of the conference, "Inspirational TVET," echoed through the hall, Kumari-Devi and Haneul-Dae's stories resonated deeply with the audience. It seems that their stories and experiences will forever be inspirational. As for the two speakers, their journeys mirrored the inspiration they found in each other, admiring each other's backgrounds and achievements. This time, they lingered in each other's company, feeling a quiet, blossoming connection they were reluctant to leave behind.

Their journeys had intertwined once, and now it seemed destined to last. Reflecting on their serendipitous meeting, they both smiled, knowing that everything began with a train to KL.

Conclusion

The dual journeys of South Korea and India from rags to riches through TVET illustrate the transformative power of strategic investment in vocational training.

The transformative power of strategic investment in TVET, combined with a long-term mindset, ensures sustained economic growth and innovation. Despite different starting points and unique challenges, both countries have successfully leveraged TVET to build robust economies and improve socio-economic conditions. Their stories provide valuable insights and inspiration for other nations aiming to enhance their TVET systems and achieve sustainable economic development.

Moving Forward:

Volume One was crafted to provide a foundational understanding of TVET and its evolution over time. The first four chapters delved into the history, nuances, and complexities of technical and vocational education that often go unnoticed. Our intention was not to overwhelm the reader with unnecessary details, but rather to offer a comprehensive perspective on the forces shaping TVET. This broad understanding is essential to help readers appreciate the profound impact of vocational education and training on societies, industries, and economies.

In Chapter 5, we provided a glimpse into Germany's highly regarded TVET system, specifically its DUAL model. This introduction is merely a starting point—a brief exploration of one of the most successful vocational education frameworks in the world. The goal is to lay the groundwork for a deeper dive into the DUAL system and its intricate workings, which we plan to explore in future volumes--We even added a very short story at the end to lighten the read.

What's Next?

As we look ahead, Volume Two will build on the themes introduced in this volume, offering a deeper exploration of specific elements of TVET and how they are implemented across various regions and industries. Key topics to be explored include:

- The TVET College: A detailed examination of a typical vocational institution in Germany, focusing on how these colleges operate and their role in shaping a skilled workforce.
- The TVET Industries: How industries collaborate with TVET systems to align training with real-world job requirements, ensuring students graduate with relevant skills for immediate employment.
- The TVET Mediators: Investigating the crucial intermediaries who bridge the gap between the supply side

(educational institutions and students) and the demand side (industries and employers) within the TVET ecosystem.

- The TVET Laws: A closer look at the regulatory frameworks and legislative policies that govern and support TVET systems globally, ensuring their sustainability and alignment with economic needs.
- The TVET Mindset: How the perception of vocational education impacts its effectiveness and how to foster a more positive view of TVET as a career pathway.
- The TVET Quality: Assessing how quality is maintained within TVET systems and the standards that ensure they remain relevant and competitive.

At TVET360, we hope that Volume One has served as a valuable resource in broadening your understanding of technical and vocational education. Our mission is to not only inform but also inspire policymakers, educators, and industry leaders to rethink how they approach vocational education. In doing so, we aim to foster systems that are more dynamic, adaptable, and aligned with the demands of an ever-changing global workforce.

We look forward to continuing this journey with you in future volumes, as we further dissect and discuss the many facets of TVET.

Thank you for joining us in this exploration of the powerful and transformative world of technical and vocational education.

Suggested Readings

Chapter 01: The TVET World

UNESCO. (2015). *Technical and Vocational Education and Training (TVET) strategy 2016-2021*. UNESCO.

- This document outlines UNESCO's strategic vision for TVET, emphasizing its role in promoting economic and social development through education and training.

Rauner, F., & Maclean, R. (Eds.). (2008). *Handbook of Technical and Vocational Education and Training Research*. Springer.

- This comprehensive reference provides an in-depth analysis of TVET systems worldwide, exploring the theoretical and practical aspects of vocational and technical education.

Cedefop. (2014). *Terminology of European education and training policy: A selection of 130 key terms*. Publications Office of the European Union.

- This glossary of TVET terms from Cedefop (European Centre for the Development of Vocational Training) explains the nuanced distinctions between various forms of vocational education across Europe.

Billett, S. (2011). *Vocational Education: Purposes, Traditions, and Prospects*. Springer.

- This book examines the different purposes and traditions of vocational education, providing insights into its role in preparing individuals for the workforce and supporting economic development.

Harris, R., & Short, T. (2013). *Workforce Development: Perspectives and Issues*. Springer.

- This text offers a detailed examination of workforce development, focusing on how TVET programs align with industry needs and contribute to a nation's economic growth.

Chapter 02: The TVET Origins

Bynum, C. W., & Hindle, B. (1993). *Craft guilds and apprenticeship in the early modern economy*. Oxford University Press.

- This book provides a detailed historical analysis of the evolution of guilds and their influence on early vocational training systems.

Epstein, S. R. (1998). Craft guilds, apprenticeship, and technological change in preindustrial Europe. *The Journal of Economic History*, 58(3), 684-713.

- Offers insights into how craft guilds structured training and influenced technological innovation in Europe during the preindustrial period.

Humphries, J., & Weisdorf, J. (2015). The wages of apprenticeship. *The Economic History Review*, 68(3), 793-817.

- Examines the role of apprenticeship systems in skill development and their economic impact during the Industrial Revolution.

Landes, D. S. (1969). *The unbound Prometheus: Technological change and industrial development in Western Europe from 1750 to the present*. Cambridge University Press.

- Discusses the transformation of vocational training systems and the impact of the Industrial Revolution on skill development and economic growth.

Verger, J. (2000). *Universities in the Middle Ages*. Cambridge University Press.

- Provides context on the role of educational institutions during the Middle Ages and how they coexisted and sometimes competed with guild-based training systems.

Chapter 03: The TVET STEPS

Billett, S. (2011). *Vocational education: Purposes, traditions, and prospects*. Springer.

- Provides an in-depth discussion of the philosophy and evolution of vocational education, offering insights into foundational theories and frameworks.

Rauner, F., & Maclean, R. (2008). *Handbook of Technical and Vocational Education and Training Research*. Springer.

- This comprehensive handbook offers research on TVET practices, strategies, and systems globally, providing a solid foundation for understanding TVET's diverse implementations.

UNESCO-UNEVOC International Centre for Technical and Vocational Education and Training. (2019). *The future of TVET teaching: Training for the changing world of work*.

- A report detailing the evolving role of TVET teachers, skills demands, and the importance of innovative training approaches.
  Retrieved from:
  https://unevoc.unesco.org/pub/tvet_teaching_future.pdf

Majumdar, S. (2011). Emerging challenges and trends in TVET in the Asia-Pacific region. In M. D. Wilson & S. N. Akbulut (Eds.), *Educational development in vocational education and training* (pp. 1-14). Sense Publishers.

- Explores regional challenges and strategies in TVET across Asia, including case studies that contextualize theoretical concepts.

European Centre for the Development of Vocational Training (Cedefop). (2015). *Briefing note: Work-based learning in Europe*.

- Discusses European approaches to integrating work-based learning in TVET systems, emphasizing the relevance of industry partnerships.
  Retrieved from:
  https://www.cedefop.europa.eu/files/9086_en.pdf

National Centre for Vocational Education Research (NCVER). (2019). *Understanding the return on investment from TVET*.

- Provides quantitative and qualitative research on the impact of TVET in terms of employability, economic growth, and workforce development.
  Retrieved from: https://www.ncver.edu.au/research-and-statistics/publications/all-publications/understanding-the-return-on-investment-from-tvet

Kuczera, M., & Field, S. (2018). *Apprenticeship and vocational education and training in Israel*. OECD Publishing.

- Offers an international perspective on TVET strategies and apprenticeship models, focusing on the successful integration of theory and practice.
  DOI: 10.1787/9789264302458-en

Chapter 04: The TVET Variants

Cedefop. (2014). *Terminology of European education and training policy: A selection of 130 key terms*. Publications Office of the European Union.

- Provides definitions and contextual understanding of various TVET models and terminology used across Europe.

Grollmann, P., & Rauner, F. (2007). *International perspectives on teachers and lecturers in technical and vocational education*. Springer.

- Explores the varying roles of TVET educators globally, providing insights into how different TVET models require unique teaching approaches.

International Labour Organization (ILO). (2010). *The role of Technical and Vocational Education and Training (TVET) in workforce development*.

- Discusses how different TVET variants contribute to workforce development and economic growth. Retrieved from https://www.ilo.org/wcmsp5/groups/public/---ed_emp/---ifp_skills/documents/publication/wcms_141223.pdf

Maclean, R., & Wilson, D. N. (2009). *International handbook of education for the changing world of work: Bridging academic and vocational learning*. Springer.

- Comprehensive guide on the global landscape of TVET, discussing the importance of different educational models and their regional implementations.

UNESCO. (2016). *Strategy for technical and vocational education and training (TVET) (2016–2021)*.

- Provides a framework for understanding how UNESCO views and categorizes TVET across different global contexts.
  Retrieved from
  https://unesdoc.unesco.org/ark:/48223/pf0000245239

World Bank. (2018). *Skills development in the digital age: Managing risks and harnessing opportunities*.

- Discusses how TVET models need to adapt to digitalization and new technologies, providing insights on aligning TVET variants with Industry 4.0.

World Federation of Colleges and Polytechnics (WFCP). (2017). *Advanced TVET: The role of professional technical education and training in addressing skills gaps*.

- Focuses on PTET and its global relevance, detailing how this model supports advanced skills development.
  Retrieved from https://www.wfcp.org/resources/advanced-tvet/

Chapter 05: The TVET "Maestro"

Federal Ministry of Education and Research (BMBF). (2015). *The German Vocational Training System: Successful in International Cooperation*. BMBF.

- This document outlines the structure and success factors of the German TVET system, providing insights into its implementation and international collaborations.

Euler, D. (2013). *Germany's dual vocational training system: A model for other countries?*. Bertelsmann Stiftung.

- A detailed analysis of Germany's dual system, its strengths, and challenges, with recommendations for adaptation in other national contexts.

Rauner, F., & Maclean, R. (Eds.). (2008). *Handbook of Technical and Vocational Education and Training Research*. Springer.

- Comprehensive research on global TVET systems, including Germany's model, and an in-depth comparison of international best practices.

Busemeyer, M. R., & Trampusch, C. (Eds.). (2012). *The Political Economy of Collective Skill Formation*. Oxford University Press.

- This book provides a political and economic analysis of the German dual system and its influence on workforce development.

Deissinger, T. (2015). *The German Dual System of Vocational Education and Training: Challenges and Future Prospects*. Journal of Education and Work, 28(1), 1-19.

- A journal article that evaluates the dual system's current state, its effectiveness, and potential areas for reform.

www.ingramcontent.com/pod-product-compliance
Lightning Source LLC
LaVergne TN
LVHW010055170826
845678LV00012B/2147

* 9 7 9 8 2 2 7 1 2 1 3 2 5 *